THE END OF CHILEAN DEMOCRACY

'THE END OF CHILEAN DEMOCRACY'

AN IDOC DOSSIER ON THE COUP AND ITS AFTERMATH

edited by Laurence Birns

(A CONTINUUM BOOK)
THE SEABURY PRESS • NEW YORK

The Seabury Press
815 Second Avenue
New York, N.Y. 10017

Copyright © 1973, 1974 by IDOC-North America, Inc.

Editor: Michael Roloff
Printed in the United States of America

The publisher extends grateful acknowledgment to the following organizations for their cooperation in the preparation of this publication: EPICA; Anti-Defamation League, B'nai B'rith; COFFLA; Latin American Bureau, U.S. Catholic Conference; Latin America Working Group, National Council of Churches; NACLA.

Library of Congress Cataloging in Publication Data

Birns, Laurence, comp.
 The end of Chilean democracy.

 (A Continuum book)
 1. Chile—Politics and government—1970-
I. Idoc. II. Title.
F3100.B57 1974   320.9'83'604   74-1112
ISBN 0-8164-9211-5
ISBN 0-8164-9212-3 (pbk.)

CONTENTS

THE END OF CHILEAN DEMOCRACY

THE SETTING

Le Monde, June 20 and 21, 1973: Chile's Ailing Revolution

PIERRE KALFON

With each new week, Chile's economic crisis is taking on such proportions that the more clear-headed supporters of Popular Unity now say that it is a matter of life and death for the regime.

Chile is racked by inflation. Until now, the illness has been endemic, and the Chileans, like other Third World inhabitants who buy more than they can sell, had come to look upon the affliction as a natural disaster for which there was no solution. But now, with a rate of 238 per cent (a world record), inflation is making inroads into the daily life of every citizen, reducing his buying power by almost 20 per cent every month.

10   Inflation explains the renewed vigor of wage claims, the strikes, the black market, the corruption, the lack of confidence, the anxieties in the army and the Church, the pointlessness of the "battle for production" as it is now waged, and above all the widening split between the left-wing and right-wing parties.

Everything began in 1970 with the first long-term policies, which were useful as far as they went. President Salvador Allende inherited production facilities which were only partially exploited. In order to ensure that they would be utilized to the full, and at the same time redistribute incomes and reduce unemployment, the government decided on a general wage increase.

This resulted immediately in a rise in demand for consumer goods and services, which in turn produced a considerable production boom. In spite of a flight of capital, which was to be expected, and an equally expected drop in private investment of about 30 per cent, the gross national product rose in 1971 by the considerable amount of 8.5 per cent, and inflation was kept down to the "reasonable" rate of 22.1 per cent. That was the year of the "Chilean miracle."

Scarcities

In fact what happened was that the Chilean middle class, thanks to the role it played in the economy, benefited more than any other social category from this favorable state of affairs, without however feeling they owed anything to Mr. Allende. On the contrary, the people who began, in December 1971, to complain of extreme scarcities, which even now do not exist, belong to the upper crust of society.

Even so, the volume of money doubled in 1971 (by 116 per cent), and doubled again in the following year. The rate of inflation for May 1972 (24.9 per cent) was higher than that of the entire year preceding. This was because the middle classes were putting into circulation their accumulated profits while making sure to pay no taxes by organizing a clandestine network to buy and sell staple goods. That is how the black market started. Under pressure of demand, "free" sector prices rose, leading in turn to higher manufacturing costs for articles with "frozen" prices. And these higher costs had to be counterbalanced by an additional issue of money.

On top of that, Chile, which nationalized its copper mines without really compensating the American companies which owned them, was beginning to feel the effects of the financial squeeze imposed on it by the United States through various international bodies. Meanwhile in London, the copper prices, vitally important as a source of currency, reached an all-time low.

Finally, in order to meet ever-increasing demand at home, Chile had to import more and more food at prices which, because of the dollar's decline and the international situation, were 40 (meat), 51 (wheat), and even 86 per cent (sugar) higher.

In 1972, imports of raw materials dropped, and industrial productivity ran out of steam, rising by a mere 2.8 per cent. Agricultural production slipped by 1 per cent. Chile, which is also saddled with the heaviest foreign debt in the world after Israel ($600 per inhabitant), had to ask for respite from the bankers of the "Paris club." But its main creditor, the United States, refused to come to any agreement unless the copper-mining companies received compensation.

This is why Mr. Allende, when he spoke at the United Nations, quoted Pablo Neruda's assessment of his country as a "silent Vietnam." Inflation is indeed only the economic after-effect of a political strangulation carried out partly from abroad by a Super Power determined to foil any fresh "rebellion" in its hunting preserves, and partly from within by a propertied class bent on hanging on to its profits.

What was first thought to be a "controlled skid" very rapidly gained a natural momentum which threw the whole economic machine into a wild spin and would seem to have escaped the control of the apprentice sorcerers in the Ministry of the Economy.

In two years, the government has pumped five times as much money into circulation. Banknotes of 500 escudos have been issued, and 1,000 escudo bills have already been printed. Chile is becoming one of the few countries in the world where the value of the dollar is rising, precisely because confidences in the country's own currency is collapsing. (The U.S. dollar is officially worth 105 escudos but fetches 1,300 on the black market). When inflation turns into hyper-inflation, and threatens to reach 300, even 400 per cent in the coming months, there can no·longer be any "reasonable" limit, and it is not even possible to carry out any useful sort of planning.

As though the economic situation were not already serious enough, its social, political, and moral consequences seem to be even worse. Inflation is hitting virtually all wage-earners; 88 per cent of office workers and 98 per cent of manual workers earn less than five times the monthly "basic wage" (the "salario vital")—set at 3,200 escudos in May), or next to nothing.

This explains the atmosphere of dissatisfaction and the present wave of strikes for wage increases—a phenomenon which the opposition is careful to exploit, when it is not actually instigating it. There is a growing scramble among the middle class, which is still a privileged category, to convert a rapidly deteriorating paper-money into personal property and real estate.

This disparity between supply and demand explains the disappearance of staple goods. People are now having to join long queues at the grocer's or the supermarket to buy sugar, oil, rice, soap, toothpaste, or knitting wool. There has even been such a shortage of flour over the last few weeks that bakers have shut shop.

On the other hand, everything that is lacking in the shops can be found, without too much difficulty, "elsewhere." Veritable "queuing professionals" have come into existence: whole families (which often come from the subproletariat) make purchases simply in order to resell at a high price, and they make more money that way than if they had a regular job. Whether as buyers or sellers, practically all Chileans are involved in the black market.

This is a dangerous situation for the government. While people spend hours queuing, the complaints fly thick and fast: "Before Allende, we could find anything, now there's nothing any more and we have to queue."

There are very few who realize that previously, a kind of rationing was imposed by level of income. When the degree of political awareness is low and exasperation is running high, anything is possible.

The problem of ensuring supplies has had the result of forcing the Chileans to organize themselves, district by district, into JAPS (committees of supplies and price control), which are becoming increasingly numerous. These JAPS, which were initiated by the government, are basically people's distributing organizations which work hand in hand with local grocers and sell, at legal prices (very low), staple goods which the government does its best to supply. The opposition immediately protested against this "control of the stomach by the state," and demanded that the "Juntas de Vecinos" (neighborhood committees of Social-Democrat coloring set up by the Frei administration), should be given the same powers.

As for the "pobladores" (inhabitants of poor suburbs), they have created in the province of Santiago—the most highly populated in the country—what they call "the first supply Soviet." They buy direct from the state distribution center (Dinac), and are already supplying 136,000 poor families.

This "direct supplies commando" is calling for a buying and distribution center for all the main food industries: the expropriation of all private distribution centers (which account for 70 per cent of the network), as well as that of all rural estates of over 100 acres, and the setting up of people's shops in the "poblaciones."

The problem of inflation, which was political in origin, has thus created fresh political problems. Popular Unity is rather ashamed of what the opposition has seized upon as a symbol of failure: and this is why it has been reluctant so far to deal openly with the inflation problem. The left-wing magazine *Chile Hoy* was the first

14   publication seriously to sound the alarm.

The first political party to react was the Communist Party. On May 30, its politburo published a long appeal, which said, among other things: "In order to save Chile, runaway inflation must be stopped." But the solutions it offered the working classes were not new: "The first priority must be production. Wage claims of individual categories must be postponed. Wages must be linked to output. Material bonuses should be granted. Each company should be self-financed."

Corruption

Two days later, the Communist Party's daily paper, *El Siglo,* courageously tackled a problem directly connected with inflation, and one which for the last few months has caused members of the Chilean left to complain, both privately and in public: corruption.

"Any all-out offensive against the enemies of the people would be quite pointless if it were not accompanied by a determination to put one's own house in order. Some Popular Unity militants are working hand in hand with the worst reactionary elements. They have no scruples about organizing a black market with the "momios" (the reactionaries), cornering all available products, and living it up. Whatever the party, membership in it cannot be a passport to dishonesty or inefficiency."

Soon after his election, President Allende said that it would be possible for people to "set foot" in his government, but not "dip their hands" in it. In fact, there have been many—particularly the "inventores" appointed by the government to manage nationalized factories—unable to resist the temptation to dip their hands into a source of easy profit by selling articles at two or three times the official price, with or without an invoice.

The real problem is to know whether the first step in the struggle against inflation should be a "battle for production." The question asked by the 2,000 workers of Mademsa, a household appliance factory which has been in the "social (nationalized) sector" for the last year, is: "What are we supposed to manufacture our goods with? The State is importing fewer and fewer raw materials because it lacks the necessary currency, and we've run out of steel.

"In order to keep ourselves busy, we've been forced to 'think up' communal, social, or cultural activities. Anyway, what's the point of all effort if the refrigerator we deliver to the store promptly vanishes into the black market at three times in price? We ought to be able to keep a watch over distribution."

A recent economic study published by the University of Chile pointed out that even after taking over 91 major companies according to the plan (something that parliament has always opposed), and even taking into account all the firms in the "social" and "mixed" sectors, the state would succeed in controlling only 31.7 per cent of industrial and 29.3 per cent of food production.

Mr. Allende is lucky enough to be able, even now, to rely on an aggressive and enthusiastic working class, which has the longest tradition of militancy in Latin America, and which, even though it feels it is being restrained "from above," does somehow understand that the present difficulties are connected with an important conflict between two kinds of society. The "class vote" of March 4, 1973, in favor of Popular Unity resulted in a distinct change in the opposition's tactics.

A year ago, Claudio Orrego, a Christian Democrat theoretician, explained that his party's strategy against the Allende Government was based on the example of the Russian army retreating before Napoleon or Hitler before launching a counterattack: "Never join battle when the enemy has all its strength at its disposal. Retreat right back to Moscow while at the same time launching disruptive and demoralizing attacks, adopt a scorched earth policy, abandon the cities until winter comes. Then is the time to attack."

This text throws light on the opposition attitude to the government. The Christian Democrats, by making an extremely opportune alliance with the traditional right, very cleverly banked on time's abrasive action, and turned the coalition's political mistakes and financial difficulties to their own advantage.

For the PDC, the "scorched earth" policy consisted of gradually letting go, for instance, of the 258 key companies which, following an "intervention" or a "requisition," have been included in the nationalized sector of the economy.

But in October 1971 a bill to reform the Constitution was put before Parliament. After a year and a half of shuttling between the Chamber of Deputies and Senate it was passed. But it has just resulted in a serious clash between the President (who vetoed the bill) and Parliament, which claims to have the right to reject such a veto through a simple majority.

The opposition's tactics aimed at demoralizing and disrupting the government have revealed themselves in even subtler ways. The non-conciliation parties as a whole rejected any change in the tax system (30 per cent of the tax revenue is provided directly by rich taxpayers, whereas 70 per cent comes from indirect taxes levied on the population as a whole).

These opposition parties refused to supply the necessary finance for the most recent wage readjustment. So once again the state had to have recourse to minting new money—with results that could be expected: a spurt in inflation, rising prices, a drop in buying power, dissatisfaction among wage-earners, strikes , and so on.

Last October, the National Party sensed it could overthrow the government by supporting the strike of shopkeepers and truckers. The PDC took the same line, but failed to persuade its troops to join battle (civil servants, scale farmers, technicians, skilled workers). The mobilization of the working classes and the unwillingness of the army to take sides made it clear that the time was not ripe.

But this time inflation, with its resultant shortages and the black market, is obviously a trump card which can be played in an attempt to cut off Popular Unity from its working-class base.

In Parliament, increased antagonism against the government has been marked by a whole series of constitutional accusations against Ministers and provincial administrators (30 in as many months), the systematic obstruction of any government project, slanging matches, and even fisticuffs.

But such excesses only tend to strengthen the widespread feeling that "the semicircle (Chamber of Deputies) is a semi-circus," and that the sort of games they are getting up to no longer have much to do with the country itself. This type of antiparliamentarianism could result in a populist totalitarianism just as easily as a fascist one.

Civil War?

The left continues to harp on the danger of civil war, and there are many comparisons with the situation in Spain in 1936, Djakarta and the massacre of communists, and even "the night of the long knives" (the slaugher of SA leaders by the SS in 1934).

The young Turks of MIR (the revolutionary left) seem to have listened docilely to Carlos Rafael Rodriguez, General Secretary of the Cuban Communist Party, who told them, on a visit to Chile, that there was no left-wing alternative to Popular Unity.

The Chilean Communist Party has not at all appreciated the way its headquarters and its militants have been attacked, nor have they taken kindly to the Christian Democrats' all-or-nothing attitude: they now no longer talk of negotiating, but of "pushing ahead without compromising."

The Socialist Party leader, Carlos Altamirano, who has just returned from Moscow, argues that the choice now lies between "socialism and fascism." He criticizes the government for not using all the power at its disposal, out of fear of a direct clash, and for thus encouraging a counter-revolutionary situation.

Last October, Mr. Allende solved the crisis by resorting to the "magic brew" of a Cabinet which included representatives of the army. Again today, the Head of State is bringing more military leaders into the government as a way of combating inflation while protecting himself from the new criticisms being levelled at his administration.

But it is not at all certain that the presence of one or two generals in the Cabinet will put the economy on its feet. Any standard disinflationary policy will inevitably involve repressive measures (whether overt or disguised) against the working classes.

Mr. Allende may perhaps hang on to the presidency, with the grudging acceptance of moderates on both sides. But whether he will salvage the Chilean "revolution" is quite another matter.

The Demise of a Constitutional Society

LAURENCE BIRNS

The following article originally appeared in the November 1, 1973 issue of The New York Review of Books *under the title "The Death of Chile." Professor Birns teaches Latin American politics at the New School for Social Research and is Editor of* IDOC. *During the first half of 1973 he was stationed in Santiago, Chile, where he was a senior economic affairs officer with the U.N.'s Economic Commission for Latin America.*

It will take years to assess all the changes that President Allende was able to make before he died, midway through his six-year term. That he had done much for Chile is beyond question. His predecessor, Eduardo Frei, only began substantial reforms after the first half of his presidency. What will now happen to these changes is still an open question. It is likely that in the repression which we are now witnessing they may be washed away.

Before I describe the benefits and some of the costs of the Allende years, I must discuss the nature and policies of the ruling military junta and the *golpe* that it staged on the eleventh of September. We had heard that Chile's armed forces were institutionally loyal; that they had accepted their place in the life of the nation and were vigorous supporters of civilian supremacy and the rule of the constitution. This was certainly true since the civil war of 1891 in which the president, Jose Manuel Balmaceda, was overthrown. That struggle, in which segments of the armed forces were pitted against each other, cost the nation 10,000 lives out of what was then a population of under two million. The landed aristocracy and the nitrate barons were temporarily successful against an apostle of middle-class reforms, but their victory was short-lived since the middle class was able to win representation in national life through electoral means. During the following decades (and then only in the depression years following World War I) the military rarely acted. When it did, it did so with self-restraint. Now the violence, the systematic terror, and the well-planned barbarism of the military have astonished students of Chilean history and sociology and made obsolete the data and assumptions with which they were working.

The full force of the repression is hard to appreciate because statistics are concealed as military secrets and few foreign reporters are able to reconstruct them. It is only clear that the killings, beatings, and arrests go on as if Chile needs a new atrocity every day to remind it that it is now under the jackboot. We hear mainly of dramatic examples: Victor Jara, the Pete Seeger of Chile, was coolly killed in the National Stadium because his protest songs angered the military mind. The universities, once among Latin America's greatest, have been taken over by the military, their principle of autonomy now a joke, their dissident faculties and students pruned according to master lists compiled by a variety of vengeance squads. The social sciences are proscribed as morally poisonous and will be replaced by such "safe" disciplines as science and technology.

For the moment the nation is entirely in the hands of the military. People are summarily dismissed from jobs because of their alleged political beliefs. Peremptory searches of neighborhoods are made at will, and their inhabitants are marched off to secret destinations. Those radio and television stations and newspapers that are permitted to operate do so under the threat of censorship; dissident books, journals, and magazines are burned or destroyed; the intellectual life of Chile is in hiding. Rather than a coup, what we have here is a *putsch*—the junta did not want merely to take over the government but to impose by terror a new system based on physical and psychological fear.

But its problems are just beginning. Obviously admiring of their military colleagues who rule in Brazilia, the junta officers must avoid too close a relation with them if they are not to offend the other Pacific Coast countries that are members of the Andean Pact. If Chile aligns itself with Brazil it will find itself estranged from the Hispanic nations, led by its traditional enemy Argentina, who fear the growing power of Brazil. Furthermore, the generals can take little comfort from recent Argentine history. For while disposing of civilian rule has been easy for the Argentine generals, they have never been able to govern in its stead. Throughout 1972 Argentine trade unions were in turmoil in Cordoba, and in Chile similar trouble could well take place in an industrial city such as Concepcion. In the same year the Argentine military caused grave shock and resentment when it massacred political prisoners in the town of Trelew; the Chilean junta has been acting with equal ferocity each day of its short period in office. By outlawing the Peronist

movements, Argentine officers only caused it to reappear
in other forms.

Argentina was ungovernable after its military overthrew
the constitutional government in 1966. How long can
Chile's armed forces remain in power? And if the
military dictators in Buenos Aires had to deliver power to
Peron because of their own political ineptitude to whom
could the Chilean generals turn over their power when
their situation becomes equally desperate, as it may well
do? None of the likely possibilities can offer them much
comfort. Two of the potential leaders are now out of the
country and a third is about to leave. The first is Carlos
Prats, the former commander-in-chief of the Chilean
army, who loyally served Allende as he would have served
any other constitutional president. When he resigned
simultaneously from the armed forces and from the
president's cabinet in August he was trying to preserve
the government and placate his colleagues. Respected by
all and feared by many of them for his philosophy of
military obedience to civilian authority, he was, in a rare
act of kindness, spared by the military when he was in its
hands. Now in Argentina, he may some day, in a symbolic if not literal sense—like O'Higgins a century and a
half ago—cross the Andes to liberate his nation.

Another choice is Gabriel Valdes, now in New York as
the director for Latin America of the United Nations
Development Program. Although he has persistently
disclaimed any political ambitions, he has many ad-
mirers among the left wing of his party. A Christian
Democrat with fierce loyalties to democratic principles
and the rule of law, he is respected throughout South
America for his advocacy of regional autonomy and
national self-development. When he was foreign minister
under Frei he insisted at the Vina del Mar conference in
1969 that Latin America declare economic independence
from the U.S.; and he continuously nettled Edward
Korry, then the U.S. ambassador, because he resisted
Korry's meddling in Chilean affairs. (Korry has now
resurfaced in New York, amazingly enough, as the
president of the United Nations Association. His part in
helping to create the conditions for Allende's downfall
should be one of the main tasks of the research that is

now commencing on the Allende years.)

A third candidate for restoring traditional democratic
rule in Chile is Radomiro Tomic, the Christian
Democratic Party's (P.D.C.) candidate in 1970. An
outspoken man who espouses both socialist ecomomics
and Christian humanism, he is loathed by many of the
middle class who feel that he helped to soften the
electorate for Allende's victory when he ran on a plat-
form similar to Allende's, including nationalization of
the major industries and confiscation of the copper
mines. But he is also widely admired as a man of probity
and intellectual consistency. He is also one of Chile's
leading social scientists and best-known university
professors.

But the military junta is not likely to transfer its new
authority to anyone. If it intends to stay in power, where
is its support?

The generals no longer lead a national army as they did
just a short period ago, but have now become the force of
the *oligarquia*, the coalition of big business and big
landowners that opposed not only Allende but the
reforms of Frei as well. I suspect that at least 40 per cent
of the population despises them, a proportion that will
grow as members of the middle class and the professions
come more and more to resent the new arrogance of the
military and the policies that it is bound to pursue. What
will the military junta do? It cannot return to its barracks
after handing back the government to the regular
political parties and parliament. It has nothing but scorn
for them. And then there is all the blood that has been
spilled, the executions by firing squads, and the torture
that has taken place. After such terror the junta cannot
summon normality as it would a class to school. But can
the junta continue to rule, supported only by discipline
and weapons?

It is now clear that the right wing of the Christian
Democrats, led by Frei, thought a military solution was
the only one feasible. They refused to work out compromises with Allende that would have kept the political
system intact. But they were thinking of the 1920's when

the military acted more gently and cleared the way for a resumption of normal political life. They seem to have forgotten the army's motto, "By reason or by force." At the beginning of the summer, General Pinochet, the leader of the junta, had proclaimed that if the military "came out" it would "kill." One cannot blame the middle class for misjudging its army; practically all Chilean experts did so too. What one can condemn them for is seeking a military solution in the first place. Why did they turn to the military? Was it because the military had guns and seemed to be apolitical? Why should Frei and his followers in the P.D.C. have expected the military to be a more patriotic custodian of the national traditions than they were themselves?

The military has taken an irrevocable step. They came out and they "killed." In a recent story on the "Slaughterhouse in Santiago," *Newsweek's* Chilean correspondent estimated that between two and three thousand people had been killed or wounded in Santiago alone. My colleagues and I, using information secretly coming out of Santiago, estimate that from seven to ten thousand people may have been killed throughout Chile, a figure that takes into account reports of the repression that has been going on in the villages of the south and north.

Most of the urban casualties were in the neighborhoods of the poor and were under-reported. Foreign newsmen could not get to see these *poblaciones* and they were therefore temporarily invisible. But in fact the *rotos*, the broken ones, had, during Allende's regime, lost the habit of accepting invisibility. Having tasted the real power that their government gave them, they can't be expected to return to their former degradation. They too can kill. At the very least they can produce a Northern Ireland. They can bomb, they can kidnap, and they can assassinate. No military force is large enough to prevent this.

But the politics of counterviolence is not all that the military faces. It is unreasonable to expect that an important faction of the P.D.C.—associates of Tomic and Valdes—will play the trained creatures of a military master. They are political men whose reformist party stood for due process and a democratic life. According to those who have been in touch with them, they, and many other members of the middle class, are appalled by the cruelty of the junta and its bold advocacy of a centurion corporate state. Already, in a statement unreported in the U.S. or Chile, but printed in the European and Latin American press, Bernardo Leighton and Renan Fuentealba, joined by other left-wing P.D.C. congressmen, attacked their own party for supporting the junta. This group will doubtless grow as the numbness wears off and they learn to live with, and master, fear. Even the editor of a right-wing newspaper recently declared that there was more press freedon under Allende than now exists. The military's fate will partly depend on the degree of terror that it is prepared to maintain. It may gain time by resorting to a policy of meticulous extermination of all opposition. But its fate will always be perilous.

In assessing the Allende years, one must recognize what he restrained his government from doing, as well as acknowledge the misdirection of some of his economic and social policies. Allende preserved the integrity of political institutions although he was thwarted by a highly political court and legislature, and in turn tried to outflank their power. There was far less intentional police brutality under Allende than existed under the previous Christian Democratic regime. There were hardly any cases of imprisonment on political grounds. The universities were entirely free although some faculties became heavily politicized. The radio and press, wretched as they were, were free to give their often hysterical versions of events from all political points of view. Political life was almost entirely free of secret police surveillance. Under Allende, politics were difficult, frustrating, sectarian, but most of all they were dangerous. It was this last element that pronounced the final sentence on the president, the Constitution, and the self-regulating apparatus of political life.

Why dangerous? Because Allende attempted to use politics to bring social justice to a nation that was lacking in it. Faced with a smug middle class that cared as little

for its poor as we do for ours, Allende attempted to undo
a system in which 5 percent of the families controlled
some 35 percent of the agricultural land, in which the
banks worked only for the established rich and industries
underproduced products that were overpriced. He attempted, and with significant success, to bring health,
housing, a better diet, and education to the poor, and a
sense of dignity and of national participation to those for
whom Chile's constitutional system had previously been
unreal and fraudulent.

Now the military junta acts as if the old script can be
replayed. The new regime's economic commissar, Raul
Saez, has recently been touted by the *Wall Street Journal*
correspondent, Everett Martin, as a no-nonsense man
who will bring Chile's economy back to normalcy. What
Martin doesn't mention is that Saez, the son of a general
who himself attempted a coup against President Ibanez,
was artfully dismissed by Frei from his position of
minister of the treasury after only twenty days because of
his harsh and inhumane proposed policies. When the
junta's new foreign minister arrived in New York, he was
accompanied by Ricardo Claro, one of the leading
members of the old group of unregenerate capitalists
who were called *las piranas* during the Frei regime. Claro
had left Chile when Allende came to power. Now he and
the rest of the *ancien regime* are back in business. Their
first customers—and they are good prospects—are Nixon
and Kissinger and their corporate allies. Already the U.S.
business community, as represented by the Council of the
Americas, which has been mute about the suppression of
human rights in Chile, has been told of the investment
opportunities in the "new" Chile at a New York meeting
addressed by the foreign minister.

A Brazilian exile, an expert on his own country's military
dictatorship, stated in early October that since 1964,
when the legal government of Brazil was overthrown,
perhaps 1,000 dissenters lost their lives. In Chile, that
figure was easily reached in a day. This was not a typical
Latin American coup. It cannot be compared to what
took place in Argentina in 1966 or Brazil in 1964. It was
more in the Iraqi or Indonesian style. It was a ruthless
move that destroyed national institutions in a far more

sweeping manner than has ever before been attempted in the modern history of Latin America.

It will be interesting to hear the comments of those who insisted that Allende didn't have a sufficient popular mandate to bring about the changes which he attempted. For the military, without any mandate whatsoever, has accomplished changes more severe than any ever dared by Allende and has wiped out any pretense at pluralism in the Chilean social system. The Church and the military class, for example, were upset by Allende's plans to unify the educational system, cutting back the role of private schools, and introducing themes of national reform and the value of manual labor into the curriculum. Although the American press barely reported them, these plans heavily contributed to the concentration of military and middle-class opposition against Allende. In fact his proposals grew out of discussions on education that have been going on for decades in Chile; they were never carried out and were undergoing modification when he fell. Now Chile has school "reforms" far more drastic than anything the Allende government ever contemplated.

The U.S. bears major responsibility for what happened in Chile. Its systematic policy of economic strangulation created a momentum which led to the death of constitutional democracy. This policy reflected the demands of the American corporations that had been nationalized or controlled in Chile. It was conceived in 1971 by John Connally when he was Secretary of the Treasury, was carried out by his assistant, John Hennessy (a man with solid Wall Street connections), and openly stated by President Nixon in January, 1972. The Chilean economy, we now might say, was sentenced to hang from its neck and turn slowly in the wind. The Nixon government exerted pressure to block Chile's customary sources of private financing and, by using the threat of a U.S. veto, it stopped Allende from getting important loans from the World Bank and the Inter-American Development Bank. Chile has classically needed foreign exchange to buy the food and other consumer goods that it has not been able to produce for itself. Cut off from the funds on which it had counted, the Allende government was unable to supply the nation's middle class with luxuries and essentials to which it was accustomed.

High inflation and economic shortages were not inaugurated by Allende's regime. Inflation has been characteristic of Chile's economy in this century and it soared during the last years of the Frei government. Although it is true Allende's attempts at nationalization and land and income redistribution were often disorganized and inefficient, it is also true that the shortages that were so irritating to middle-class Chileans would have been much less severe if Allende had not been prevented by the U.S. from getting U.S. foreign loans and hard currency. Deprived and then embittered, the middle-class opposition parties repeatedly pressed the military to do its duty and come out of the barracks. Even if we grant that grievous mistakes were made in social and economic policy, to justify destroying a constitutional government because of such errors would be unthinkable in any western democracy. Yet this is precisely what the *Wall Street Journal* and Graham Hovey in his editorials in *The New York Times* have been doing, as they construct a mythology designed to show that Allende was responsible for his own fall, however lamentable the result. We may soon expect to hear roughly the same language from Secretary of State Kissinger, one of the principal architects of the "get Chile" policy.

This should not surprise us. Under the Nixon administration there are fewer democratic regimes in Latin America than there have been for decades. Aside from the *Washington Post* and Senators Kennedy and Church, and a few others, hardly anyone in Washington, Democrat or Republican, seems to care when democratic social reform is subverted and when the aims of a handful of U.S. corporations are transmuted into U.S. foreign policy. By placing private interests above the survival of democratic institutions in Chile, our government has directly contributed to the death of yet another free government in the hemisphere.

THE COUP AND ITS AFTERMATH

The farewell speech by President Salvador Allende was made on the morning of the military coup from his quarters in the presidential palace, the Moneda. Shortly afterwards he was to die in this building after the palace was bombed by the Chilean air force and subjected to a tank attack by the army. Luis Renato Gonzales Cordoba, a member of the President's coterie, gives an eye-witness account of these events as they unfolded in the Moneda on that September the eleventh. The statement made by Admiral Ismael Huerta, the foreign minister of the military junta, is a defense of the actions taken by the new government and an attack against the Allende government. Jonathan Kandell's New York Times *article, if upheld by future investigation, is of critical importance for it maintains that the plotting of the coup began almost a year before it was staged, and was not necessarily a response to any particular provocation by the Allende government. Richard Gott's article is a critical analysis of the policies put into effect by the military. The cable sent by Luis Ramallo played a key role in enabling* Newsweek *magazine to support the claim made by its correspondent John Barnes in its issue of*

30 *October 8, 1973, that the Santiago morgue was processing large numbers of bodies of people killed by the military in the coup's aftermath. The* Wall Street Journal, *in its issue of November 2, denied the validity of these figures and suggested that the actual number of casualties caused by the coup was relatively low. A dramatic meeting between Barnes and Ramallo took place in the IDOC office, where they substantiated each other's account. Based on this interview and the existence of the Ramallo telegram, which had been independently sent before the Barnes account had been published,* Newsweek *was able to put forth a strong defense in space donated by the* Wall Street Journal *on November 15, 1973.*

President Allende's Last Address

The following is the complete text of President Salvador Allende's farewell speech to the nation which was carried over Radio Magallenes on the morning of September 11, 1973. It was obtained from COFFLA, which also did the translation.

Surely this will be the last opportunity I will have to address myself to you. The air force has bombed the towers of Radio Portales and Radio Corporacion. My words do not come out of bitterness, but rather deception, that they may be the moral punishment for those who betrayed the oath they took as soldiers of Chile, titular commanders in chief . . . Admiral Merino, who has self-designated himself commander of the armada . . . Mr. Mendoza, the callous general who only yesterday declared his loyalty to the government, has been named director-general of the carabineros (Chilean National Police).

In the face of these facts, the only thing left for me to say to the workers: I will not resign! Placed in a historical transition, I will pay with my life for the loyalty of the People. I say to you that I have the assurance that the seed that we plant in the dignified consciousnesses of thousands and thousands of Chileans cannot be forever blinded.

They have the power, they can smash us, but the social processes are not detained, neither with crimes, nor with power. History is ours, and the People will make it.

Workers of my country: I want to thank you for the loyalty which you always have shown, the trust which you placed in a man who was only the interpreter of the great desires of justice, who gave his word that he would respect the Constitution and the law, and that I did.

In this definitive moment, the last thing which I can say to you is that I hope you will learn this lesson: foreign capital, imperialism united with reaction, created the climate for the armed forces to break with their tradition, that of General Schneider, and which Commander Araya reaffirmed, a victim of the same social sector which today finds them in their houses, waiting to retake power, by strange hands, to continue defending their huge estates and privileges.

I address myself above all to the modest woman of our land, to the peasant woman who believed in us, to the working woman who worked more, to the mother who knew of our concern for her children. I address myself to the professionals of our land, to the patriotic professionals, to those who were working against the auspicious sedition carried out by the professional schools, schools of class which also defend the advantages which capitalist society gives them.

I address myself to the youth, to those who sang, who gave their joy and spirit to the struggle. I address myself to the Chilean man: to the worker, the peasant, the intellectual, to those who will be persecuted because fascism has already been present in our country for many hours: those terrorist actions which blew up bridges, cutting railway lines, destroying oil and gas pipelines, in the face of the silence of those who had the obligation of pronouncing themselves. History will judge them.

Probably Radio Magallanes will be silenced, and the calm metal of my voice will not reach you: it does not matter. You will continue to hear me, I will always be beside you or at least my memory will be that of dignified man, that of a man who was loyal.

Workers of my country: I have faith in Chile and in her destiny. Other men will overcome this grey and bitter moment where treason tries to impose himself. May you continue to know that much sooner than later the great avenues through which free men will pass to build a better society will open.

Long live Chile! Long live the People! Long live the Workers!; these are my last words. I am sure that my sacrifice will not be in vain; I am sure that it will at least be a moral lesson which will punish felony, cowardice and treason.

Chile's Armed Forces

Military Service: 1 year; Total armed forces: 60,000; Estimated GNP in 1972: $7.07 million; Defence budget 1973: 8,000 million escudos ($174 million)*

Army: 32,000

5 divisions including:

6 cavalry regiments (2 armoured, 4 horsed)

16 infantry regiments (including 10 motorized)

5 artillery regiments

some anti-aircraft and support detachments

76 M-4 *Sherman* medium tanks; 10 M-3 *Stuart* light tanks; some Armoured Personnel Carriers, Model 56 105mm pack howitzers, anti-aircraft artillery.

Reserves: 200,000

Navy: 18,000

2 submarines

3 cruisers

4 destroyers

3 destroyer escorts

4 motor torpedo boats

1 patrol vessel

5 landing ships

(2 *Oberon*-class submarines and 2 *Leander*-class frigates with *Seacat* surface-to-air missiles are on order.)

1 HUO16C *Albatross*

5 C-45 and 5 C-47 transports; 4 *Jet Ranger* helicopters

Air Force: 10,000; 41 combat aircraft

1 light bomber squadron with 12 B-26 *Invaders*

2 fighter squadrons with 18 *Hunter* F-71 and 11 F-80C

About 90 transports, including 20 C-45, 8 DHC-6 *Twin Otter*

9 Beechcraft 99A, 25 C-47, 4 C-118, 4 DC-6, and 2 C-130E *Hercules*

5 *Twin Bonanza,* 10 Cessna 180, 4 Cessna 0-1 and 20 T-6 liaison aircraft

45 T-34, 10 T-37B, 8 T-33A, and 5 *Vampire* trainers

30 helicopters, including 7 Bell OH-13H, 2 Sikorsky UH-19

16 Hiller OH-23G, and 2 Bell UH-1D

Carabineros: 30,000 (para-military forces)

Source: *The Military Balance, 1973-1974.* The Institute of Strategic Studies, London.

*July 1972, 28 escudos= **$1.00**
July 1973, 46 escudos= **$1.00**

The Scene from Within the Moneda

LUIS RENATO GONZALEZ CORDOBA

The following account was taped by Mr. Gonzalez in the Mexican Embassy in Santiago shortly after he had sought refuge there. It should be noted that some events it relates and a number of deaths that it claims are contradicted by other sources. It was secured through COFFLA, a Washington-based organization, which also did the translation.

About 6:10 in the morning the Chief of the Police advised the President in Tomas Moro [the President's home] that military forces from the regiments Guardia Vieja, Paz, and naval troops were advancing toward the Moneda.

The Doctor Allende, as soon as he was informed, woke everyone in the security force so that they could immediately take up their combat positions. The vehicles were ready to escort the President to the Moneda. When we got there we met the policemen in the Palace Guard. We had to knock loudly on the doors for them to let us in. Then the Doctor called us all together and told us that the time to confront the golpistas [roughly translated means those who make the coup] and to defend our revolutionary process had come, if necessary, at the cost of our lives. With these words, the President's Guard was formed and the combat posts were designated: riflery, heavy arms, and anti-tank.

After all this the Doctor made the rounds of the Moneda to plan its defense. While making the rounds, the Doctor met with military liaison men. Two, who had always been loyal to him, asked to fight with him. To this the Doctor responded that given the treason to his government and the constitution, it was not a moment to trust in the military. Still the men did not want to leave and the Doctor ordered them, shouting, to leave the Moneda. They continued protesting and finally the Doctor took up his gun and forced them to leave by the front door.

When the liaison men had left, the Doctor went back to his rounds, checking out all areas of the Moneda. He talked to Tomas Moro by the direct line, to ask about the situation there. He also spoke to the First Lady, Dona Hortensia Bussi de Allende and told her that she should not leave Tomas Moro, that he had confidence in the security force and the guards who were ready to defend the residence.

At 8:55 Allende met with the upper commands of the police; there were no positive results. The Palace Guard of the Police decided to leave the Moneda. The Doctor ordered them out with a machine gun, so that none would stay and fight against the President from within. There was division among the upper commands which led to chaos in the Moneda. Nothing came out well. On the contrary, only a minimum part of the Palace Guard, about five men, decided to defend the Moneda. The rest were not loyal; they wanted to commit treason, to take over the Moneda.

After all this—it was already 9:20 in the morning—the first shots were heard. Without any previous ultimatum they simply began to fire with heavy artillery at 9:30 and tanks at 9:50. The infantry advanced with them. On the face of this, the Palace Guard also opened fire in response to our President's call to defend the revolutionary process, the law, and the Constitution. The firing grew more and more intense. About 30 soldiers fell, hit by our first volley. The military responded to our fire with panic and retreated to the other end of the Plaza Constitucion, returning with two heavy artillery tanks. We were ordered to fire the bazookas at the tank. The tank, No. E28, was totally destroyed on the corner of Morande and Moneda. This went on until about 11:00 in the morning, when we heard on the radios within the Moneda that the women inside the Moneda would have three minutes to abandon the Palace. They were given over to the custody of the military. After this, when all the women had left, a new message was heard over the radios, demanding the surrender of the Moneda, of the President, and its personnel. The President firmly said no, that his mission and his promise to the people was to die in the Moneda and that he would not leave it alive, nor surrender.

After a lapse of time, we heard the first airplanes. They circled the Moneda three times, around noon, and dropped their first bombs on the palace. We had to take refuge in the basement or in the stairwells between floors. Given the circumstances, the gravity of the bombing, President Allende ordered us not to lose our nerve during the bombardment. While the planes returned to their bases, combat began against the infantry, which was outside trying to enter.

The companeros, all those who were there, along with some of the companeros from investigations who were there with us, and the President's personal guard, had to double our efforts. We did not retreat for the following reason: we saw the surety of our President and his firm decision not to surrender but to fall for his government, to defend his people to the ultimate consequences, so that we did not retreat although we could have done so. But when we saw the bravery with which our President defended himself, taking his combat position as one more citizen and revolutionary, many companeros fell at his side, died without questioning, without doubt, fighting as he himself fell there assassinated, machine-gunned by the military.

In these moments, the planes returned to bombard the Moneda, dropping three bombs on their second trip. They destroyed the Patio de las Naranjas (the garden of the orange trees), the Ministry of the Interior, the reflecting pool in the Patio Colonial, and some of the conference rooms. Our companion in arms was designated Commandante Allende. He gave the orders to advance and the orders to fire within the Moneda and at the military outside, because the infantry was also trying to enter the Moneda from Teatinos and from the Alameda.

Immediately he found his daughters, Beatriz and Isabel, whom, as a father, he ordered to leave. They didn't want to and said they were ready to die with him. He said it would be worth more if they left. They still didn't want to and so he made them, using his gun, leave the Moneda. They left from the main door.

After this there was a cease fire on both sides. We met and the President said that he was determined not to surrender but to die at our sides. To this, our response was unanimous: to die together there, defending the revolutionary process. This was when he told us, "Thus is written the first page of this story. My people will write the rest."

After a lapse of five minutes, the firing from the artillery and tanks began again, which destroyed the whole facade which faces the Plaza de la Constitucion. A doctor from the Central Emergency Hospital was taken care of in the improvised clinic which we set up in the basement of the Moneda. There were three doctors in charge: Danilo, Oscar and Carlos.

Again the airplanes returned to bomb. They dropped six bombs and gravely wounded one of our companeros, Diego, who was taken to the clinic. We reopened fire towards the Plaza Constitucion where there was the greatest concentration of the infantry. They shot at all the windows which faced the living rooms of President Allende. Amidst the firing, we were able to hear one of the radios, broadcasting a petition from the golpistas which asked for a parley. Commandante Allende designated Daniel Vergara and Fernando Flores to leave the Moneda and talk with the golpista officers. It was 1:00 P.M. when they left. A tank and a military jeep waited outside Morande 80. They talked, and as Daniel Vergara and Fernando Flores walked back towards Morande 80, the fascists and traitors shot them in the back. Flores received a shot in the right thigh and vergara received four shots at the waist. The Palace Guard opened machine gun fire to cover them. The companeros who rescued them practically crawled in by the door of Morande 80 with Vergara and Flores. Once within the Moneda, Vergara said that the golpista officers wanted the surrender of Allende, and all civilian personnel with him and that they would provide a plane to leave Chile. To this the companero President said, "My firm decision is to fight and die here at my post, the Moneda." Keeping his firmness, he gave the order to reopen fire against the golpistas. It was an all-out attack, everyone fired, Augusto Olivares fell, dead. Also dead were sixteen soldiers at the doors of Morande 80.

The military, because of the deaths at the doors, installed a tank. Jointly with this tank, another tank bombarded the windows of the second floor which faces the Plaza Constitucion. Another tank was facing the main door.

Again they began to bombard the Moneda. This time the whole building began to burn. We began to suffer from asphyxiation. We had to use all the equipment the police had stored in the Moneda. We went to the armory where, in order to defend ourselves, we had to dynamite the doors in order to get at the helmets, gas masks, munitions, and heavy weapons—gas bombs, grenades, etc.—everything that would help us go on fighting. This time the firing was more intense on both sides. The golpistas opened fire with cannons, armored vehicles and machine guns. There was also firing from all the buildings surrounding the Moneda, where there were loyal companeros defending the revolutionary process. The golpistas intensified their firing at the Ministry of Public Works, where one of our companeros, Rudolfo, died. Then they bombed the City Hall to destroy it.

One of the tanks was finally able to break down the door of Morande 80. The golpistas entered the building and battles broke out in the halls, basement, and in all of the Moneda. Victor, a companero, was shot and killed. In this moment the infantry attacked in order to take over the Moneda. A large group entered from Teatinos, and the companero President decided to defend that area.

The firing within the Moneda grew more and more intense; already the golpistas had installed heavy artillery within the building. We went to take up our combat positions.

The telephones began to ring insistently one more time. Doctor Allende answered and talked with Augusto Pinochet. Pinochet asked for the surrender of Dr. Allende. He answered that he would uphold his decision to defend the revolutionary process at the cost of his life if it was necessary. He said that he would not parley with traitors to the law, the Constitution, and the nation. He then hung up very angry. We then went to our combat positions. The military forces who entered the Moneda were machine-gunned by the forces that were defending the Moneda. The order to fire had been given by the President of the Republic, Dr. Salvador Allende Gossens. This fight lasted about an hour.

Once we had retreated to other combat positions, we encountered a group of fascists under the command of Captain Mayor, in the halls near the Red Room. He shouted: "Surrender, Senor Allende." Our companero said, "Never. It is better to leave dead than surrender." When he finished we heard a shot from the military. It hit the Doctor. They opened machine gun fire, and we fired against them. Twelve of our companeros fell dead at the side of President Salvador Allende. Our firing became more intense. The officer and six soldiers fell. We approached the President's body. He was mortally wounded. He told us, "A leader may fall, but still there is a cause. America will be free." It was 1:50 P.M. when companero Allende fell, assassinated by the bullets of the fascists and traitors. He had been hit by about six bullets; four in the neck and two in the thorax.

After this we began our painful task. We picked up his martyred body and took it to its place, the Presidential Office. We sat him in his seat, put his Presidential banner on, his gun in his arms, and embraced him. We found the flag, for which he had fought so hard, at his right. We took it off its pole and covered his body in it. In tears, impotent and enraged, we left him. But we kept on fighting and firing, trying to eliminate the fascist scum.

In the hallway we ran up against a strong military contingent which forced us to give up our arms. We were beaten, clubbed, and kicked. They pushed and shoved us out of the door of Morande 80. There they continued beating us and torturing us cruelly. After that we were lying on the ground; an officer ordered a tank to run over us, but another officer opposed him. Then from the Ministry of Public Works someone fired on the officer who wanted the tanks to run us over and he was gravely wounded. The soldiers began to run over us. If we moved, they clubbed and kicked us. An officer gave an order that they take away the Marxist dogs who were injured. Among those who were arrested and lying on the ground were: Lapajaita, Allende's personal secretary, the wife of Minister Carlos Riego. The ambulances arrived and they took away all the companeros with bullet wounds. Some of them were taken to the Central Emergency Hospital, others to the military school. Among those who were taken to the military school were Minister Fernando Flores and Minister Carlos Riego. When an officer was informed that Daniel Vergara was gravely wounded, Vergara was clubbed and assassinated by the military on the spot.

While we were lying on the ground, one of our companeros with a white handkerchief came out of the Public Works Ministry with his hands up. They shot him and he fell, riddled with bullets. As we asked who it was, we realized it was Anibal Palma Sucada. Jose Toha was taken from a nearby building, with a bullet wound; his brother Jaime was found inside it. Those assassinated in the Moneda were: Victor, Rodolfo, Carlos, and Ignacio, companero Augusto Olivares who was hit about fifteen times, and companero Daniel Vergara who was fighting in the Moneda and was assassinated as I mentioned before. The military lost more than a hundred men plus two tanks semi-destroyed and one totally destroyed. Also a plane was hit and had to return to its base.

In Defense of the Junta

ADMIRAL ISMAEL HUERTA

This is the statement presented by the ruling Junta's Minister for Foreign Affairs. Vice-Admiral Huerta, before the General Assembly of the United Nations on October 9, 1973. It has been slightly abridged.

This is the first opportunity that the present government of Chile has had to state from the highest world rostrum the background and the facts that led the armed forces and police to take control of power and establish a regime of national restoration and dignity. I shall deal at some length with the subject, although I am aware that one of the fundamental principles of the Charter is that the United Nations shall not intervene in affairs that are essentially within the domestic jurisdiction of states. That principle, which also governs bilateral relations among members of the international community, is one to which I will refer more especially later.

However, due to the events that have taken place in Chile, a campaign that is so false, so distorted, so vicious, so well orchestrated has been launched with the intention of distorting the facts and the intentions of the government, that I felt it both fitting and proper to refer to those events, even though I firmly contend that no state, and no international organization, has the right to meddle in or judge what has taken place in my homeland.

I understand that the events that have taken place in

Chile have not left world opinion indifferent. Although many countries in the very different regions of the world year after year, for different reasons, undergo changes in their political and social life, the case of Chile is a very special one, for two reasons. The first is that my country, after more than a century and a half of independence, has stood as an example of civic life and has never tolerated dictatorship, racism or totalitarism, and that our eminently apolitical and professional armed forces have been an example to the world. We who wear uniforms are proud of that tradition.

Secondly, Chile, having agreed to the establishment by democratic means of a government imbued with foreign doctrines, loyally collaborated in the search for a socialist direction compatible with our own national reality and our traditions of freedom, justice and dignity. This was so much so that, at the beginning of the socialist experiment, the political parties as a whole supported the government as in the nationalization of the copper industry, and thus, when in moments of grave crisis the armed forces also assumed a heavy responsibility upon their shoulders, it was with unanimous support.

But these generous, democratic and selfless attitudes proved futile, since they were only able briefly to contain, and not stop, the disastrous course towards which the Unidad Popular, in its eagerness to consolidate a tyrannical position, was forcing the country. Chile, alone, without the help or inspiration of any, its patience exhausted and drawing on its courage, drive and inner resources that are a feature of our people, was able to react and put an end to the totalitarian system that had subjugated so many countries of the world, before it was too late.

I shall refer to what happened in my country three years ago.

In September 1970, Chile was confronted with a procedure that was normal in our history of democracy: a presidential election was to be held. On 4 September the candidate representing the Unidad Popular won 36.2 per cent of the popular vote in a free, democratic election,

44   precisely in keeping with the historic traditions of Chile.

This triumph was a surprise and upset to the majority of the people, since the ideology professed by the winning candidate made many of my countrymen fear that the country might adopt a course very contrary to the tradition and history of Chile.

Under the political Constitution of the State, the election had to be ratified by the National Congress, since none of the candidates had obtained an absolute majority of the popular vote. The political parties that had supported the Marxist candidates were a minority in the Chilean Congress and thus, interpreting the national feeling, the majority political parties conditioned the ratification of the candidate obtaining a relative majority, out of solemn respect for the provisions of the Constitution, supplemented by a special Statute of Guarantees.

From the very dawn of our independent life, Chile has been careful to preserve, both in reality and in our fundamental Constitution, the basic human rights of the individual and respect for the common good. In the case of the Unidad Popular candidate, the majority parties insisted that these guarantees be more specifically confirmed through the supplementary Statute to which I referred earlier. As a result of this requirement on the part of the parliamentary majority, the National Congress unanimously, and with the favourable vote of the candidate himself, approved constitutional reforms that tended primarily to reaffirm the independence of the armed forces and the respect for their professional function. This stood in the way of the creation of military groups outside the Constitution and the law. This also reaffirmed the freedom of the media, reaffirmed the political rights of citizens and the attainments won by the workers in organized labor , and ensured the participation of professionals, technicians, experts, employees and workers in the process of economic development.

It was only after the approval of this Statute of Constitutional Guarantees that the congressional majority which, I repeat, had opposed the posture of the Unidad

Popular candidate, agreed to confer upon him the Presidency of Chile.

The Chilean political system is based upon the absolute independence of the public authorities and upon their unlimited mutual respect. The President of the Republic, the National Congress and the Courts of Justice, in the political Constitution of the State, have specifically defined rights and powers and the way in which they shall relate to one another.

Furthermore, there must be added the fundamental role played in the Chilean legal system by the Comptroller-General of the Republic, since his decisions and resolutions determine the administrative process of the nation.

In other words, when the legitimately elected President took over the highest office in Chile, he agreed under oath to respect the independence and authority of the other institutions of the State. He committed himself to respect the legality of the Chilean State, the heritage of the people which in the course of years has moulded into a general system of coexistence among them all.

Any attempt, therefore, against the legality of the country is a destruction not only of the cultural and moral heritage of the nation, but denies any possibility of democratic life.

In a veiled and surreptitious way at first, but quite openly later, the government entirely ignored all the basic principles that I have enunciated here and, what was even more serious, repeatedly violated the constitutional provisions that the National Congress had demanded as a guarantee after the elections of September 1970.

The bare-faced way in which the government was acting was amply demonstrated when the chief of state later made known in a press interview that he had accepted the Statute of Constitutional Guarantees as a tactical necessity to assume power, and that was what was most important at the moment was to take over the government.

46   Under the tolerant eyes of the government, the free press was harrassed and, instead of implementing the agrarian reform laws drawn up by the previous administration, an illegal system of alienation and takeovers was established. Authorities arbitrarily took over small, middle and large-scale industries; politicians, villagers, students and representatives of law and order were assassinated with impunity. Labour leaders and union representatives who did not support the government were persecuted and jailed, and an attempt was made to impose a totalitarian educational system on all Chilean children.

I think a separate mention must be made of the government's attitude towards the armed groups of civilians. It not only permitted them, but openly encouraged them and thus illegally allowed the entry into the country of foreign agitators and weapons. By 11 September this year, more than 13,000 known foreigners, most of them extremists, were known to be in the country in an illegal manner. Their sole mission was to set up a parallel army to oppose the regular armed forces. Representatives in the Assembly can well understand what the number of persons could mean to a country with 10 million inhabitants. But the conduct of those foreigners went even further. They took over management positions in the offices of public administration, in illegally sequestered factories and in the direction of the national economy. We saw—with shame, I admit—how foreigners became part of Chilean delegations entrusted with the task of negotiating international agreements.

But to all this must yet be added the inability of the government to draw up an economic plan that would meet our real national needs, and this failure led to the catastrophe from which Chile will not recover for many years. The economic experience of Marxism in our country, because of the damage it has done, will be difficult for our countrymen to forget.

Let me cite a few figures to support what I am saying.

According to the latest official statistics of the government of the Unidad Popular, agricultural production dropped by 20 per cent last year; industrial production by 9 per cent; and mineral exports, the fundamental mainstay of our economy, by 28 per cent.

In 1970, the total currency in circulation in Chile was 12,114 million escudos. At the end of this year, according to projections, the currency in circulation will be about 23 times greater.

In 1970, Chile's external debt was U.S. $2,630 million. By 31 December 1973, that debt will have reached U.S.$ 3,450 million. And, to make things worse, this increase in foreign indebtedness was due primarily to the import not of capital goods destined to increase production, but of food and other perishables which the Marxist economy had been unable to produce for the country.

In 1970, Chile's trade balance showed a surplus of U.S.$78 million. Thus far this year, our balance of payments shows a deficit of U.S.$438 million; and to this must be added the fact that under the management of the Unidad Popular government the country lost its entire reserves of foreign exchange, which in 1970 had reached U.S.$448 million.

In 1972, the deficit in fiscal expenditure amounted to 40 per cent of the total budget. For this year, it is estimated that the deficit will surpass 50 per cent of total public expenditure.

All these economic facts led the country to sustain the highest inflation rate in the world: 323 per cent over the last 12 months.

In March of this year, under the control of the armed forces, as required by law, normal parliamentary elections took place; although it was later discovered that the voting registers had been cleverly altered and tampered with. Nevertheless, those elections clearly and precisely confirmed the fact that the government of the Unidad Popular could count on the support of only a minority in the country. The opposition parties obtained a wide majority in the Senate and in the Chamber of Deputies.

48   The government was careful to demonstrate apparent respect for the judicial branch for the benefit of the outside world. It is true, it took pains not to interfere visibly with the structure itself; but it drew upon all sorts of resources in order to undermine the hard-won prestige of the judiciary as the guardian of civil rights. It had no compunction about carrying out defamatory campaigns; its officers indulged in all sorts of disrespectful acts, and sentences were deprived of all meaning when the government disregarded them, whenever it suited the partisan interests of the government of the Unidad Popular. Moreover, the power to grant amnesty was abused in the most inconceivable manner and the courts were denied the public force to carry out their functions.

Time and time again, the Supreme Court entered its protests, but the government, far from changing its mistaken plan of action, pushed harder and harder, until the Court ultimately, in communication with the President of the Republic, felt obliged to denounce these events as conducive to "a crisis in the legal system about which this Tribunal cannot keep silent." That was a warning from the Supreme Court.

The abuse of the law became even worse, when last May, in a note to the Chief of State, the Supreme Court stated publicly something that was even more serious: namely, that the country was faced with "a peremptory and imminent breakdown of the legal system."

And yet, the government continued with its policies, and the Chief of State even tried to justify them by instigating a public polemic with the Supreme Court, which only succeeded in reinforcing the Court's original position.

But the judiciary was not the only institution that had to try to defend the public interest and to point to the serious misdirection of the government the Office of the Comptroller-General of the Republic was also object of increasingly inflammatory attacks and repeated slights. The government abused the instrument of "mandatory decrees," thus implementing a ruling system bypassing Congress; and the President of the Republic even went so far as to ignore the opinion of the Comptroller-General when it came to the promulgation of a constitutional reform approved by the Parliament, which the Executive proposed to enact only partially.

After fighting hard to find a political way to protect the national interest, Parliament itself finally assumed a position comparable to that of the judicial branch and of the Comptroller-General of the Republic. Even the possibility of submitting the government to a plebiscite was rejected by the Unidad Popular, thus proving its lack of democratic support even more openly.

On 22 August last, the Chamber of Deputies, which is the controlling branch of Congress, clearly and energetically denounced the government's headlong path to destruction. By 81 votes to 47, the Chamber adopted a very important resolution, the main points of which I should like to quote.

To begin with, the resolution pointed out that sovereignty lies essentially in the nation; that the authorities can only exercise powers delegated by the nation, and that a government, by assuming rights not conferred by the people, is liable to charges of sedition. The resolution went on to declare:

> It is a fact that the present government of the Republic, since its inception, has been engaged in the conquest of total power with the obvious intention of subjecting all persons to the strictest state economic and political control in order thus to achieve the installation of a totalitarian system absolutely opposed to the representative, democratic system established by the Constitution.

And, it added:

> To accomplish this objective, the government has not violated the law and the Constitution in isolated instances; rather, these violations have become permanent policy, to the extreme of ignoring systematically and attacking the characteristics of the other branches of the government, of continually violating the guarantees that the Constitution assures to every inhabitant of the Republic, and of allowing and

sheltering the creation of illegitimate parallel powers that constitute a grave danger to our institutions and to our government of law.

The Chamber of Deputies also indicated that the government had committed *inter alia* the following violations and abuses:

It has usurped the principal function of Congress, that is to legislate upon adopting a series of highly important measures for the economic and social life of the nation, which are indubitably a matter of law by mandatory decrees abusively issued or by simple administrative rulings based on legal loopholes. It must be stressed that all this has been done with the deliberate and acknowledged purpose of changing the features of the nation's structures recognized by the law in force and by the sole will of the legislative branch.

It has continually mocked the functions of control of the National Congress by depriving of all real effect congressional measures to dismiss from office cabinet ministers who violate the Constitution or the law or who commit other crimes or abuses stressed and listed in the Constitution.

And, what is most extraordinarily serious of all, it has done away with the high function of the Congress as legislative power by refusing to enact the constitutional reform covering the three areas of the economy, which was approved in strict accord with the rulings established by the Constitution.

But the agreement of the Chamber of Deputies did not stop there. It went on to enumerate the government's principal abuses of the fundamental guarantees and rights afforded by the Constitution of Chile, and, furthermore, added:

In case of breakdown of the government of law, the formation and development of armed groups under government protection is especially serious since, apart from being a danger to persons and the security of individuals and their rights and against the internal peace of the nation, such groups are intended to confront the regular armed forces. It is also extremely serious that the police force is kept from performing its most important function in the face of criminal attacks perpetrated by violent groups supporting the government.

For their grim importance, notorious and public attempts to use the armed forces and the police force for partisan purposes cannot be silenced; neither can attempts to break down their institutional hierarchy and politically infiltrate their ranks.

For the benefit of the Executive, the Chamber of Deputies' resolution closed with a description of the serious breakdown of constitutional and legal order that affected the Republic and the need immediately to rectify the situation, the urgency of channelling the actions of the government in a lawful direction and the need to ensure constitutional order in Chile.

As I have already pointed out, it was a long wait for the citizenry and the other branches of the government, who were always ready to facilitate solutions whereby to overcome the situation. As I have mentioned, the armed forces also loyally and professionally collaborated with the government. Their mission was stretched beyond the limits of their vocation, since a number of times they were required to assume responsibilities with serious political consequences. Thus, in October 1972, confronted by a tenacious civil strike and in order to calm public opinion and guarantee parliamentary elections scheduled for six months later, representatives of the Chilean army, navy and air force assumed cabinet posts. I myself acted as Minister of State at that time and bent every effort loyally and efficiently to fulfill the missions entrusted to me by the President of the Republic.

Ministers, members of the armed forces, repeatedly tried to convince the Chief of State of the need to adopt measures that might modify the course of the nation. We did achieve some revisions, but everything was erased once our mission of ensuring fair and honest elections had been accomplished, and we surrendered our cabinet posts.

After the elections of March of this year, and in order to comply with our sacred obligation to preserve the democratic system, we repeatedly tried to convince those in charge of the country of the extremely dangerous path they were following. We were answered with promises that were always broken and with assurances that bore absolutely no relation to reality.

While astute campaigns were organized to prevent a possible civil war, surreptitiously professional agitators, weapons and other highly divisive and destructive elements continued to enter the country with the specific purpose of preparing for the bloody *coup de grace* to our democratic system. I shall not tax the patience of the Assembly by describing the entire background that proves this. The reserves and deposits of weapons and explosives; clandestine hospitals and blood banks; plans for violence, assassination, sabotage; the division of the armed forces and the organizing of mercenaries and guerillas—all showed us that the abyss towards which our country was headed was far deeper than we had discovered when we adopted the historic resolution of 11 September.

It was not only the knowledge of those threatening plans that moved the armed forces and the police force of Chile to adopt the decision imposed upon us by our oath to protect the homeland.

With public opinion demoralized by so much abuse and so many threats upon their lives, humiliated by so much illegal and discriminatory rationing, and ruined by a blackmarket directed and organized by government supporters, a strike erupted in one of the great copper mines. It lasted 74 days, and was followed by a civilian uprising of vast proportions. The truckers' union, the professional associations, retailers, large groups of craftsmen, workers and laborers, still not intimidated by foreign slogans, joined to protest with the only weapon they still possessed: the paralysing of the country. And in that historic uprising of the civilian masses, noble and true to their traditions, the long suffering Chilean women rose together with important groups of young students.

The situation was becoming extremely dangerous and the government, incapable of solving any problems and basically oriented towards the seizing of total power through violence, once again resorted to the patriotism of the armed forces and the police force of Chile. Once again those of us in uniform gave generous assistance by assuming cabinet posts. From the vantage point of our high offices, we were very soon able to confirm the speed with which the country was heading towards total chaos. We noted the deep deterioration of national security. The irritating injustice of a regime that called itself "popular" while its leaders lived in ostentatious luxury, outraging the people who had to form long queues for food, was brought home to us. We could prove too the extremely dangerous level of foreign intervention in our affairs, as well as the way in which bands of authentic delinquents prepared to administer the final blow to all of those who were not already unconditionally enslaved.

Crime increased from day to day. One high naval officer, aide-de-camp to the President, was the fatal victim of a nefarious attack; a young army officer was assassinated by a foreign extremist; military intelligence services uncovered criminal acts of subversion within the ranks of the navy, instigated by important members of the regime, including the Secretary-General of the Socialist Party, to which the President himself belonged.

Our final effort to participate in the Cabinet of the deposed government did not successfully prevent the avalanche of events. Civic protest did not cease; the danger of a confrontation between the majority of the unarmed citizens and the strong paramilitary cells organized by Unidad Popular, which had drawn up a plan to assassinate civilian and military authorities and thus assume power completely, made it imperative for the armed forces and the police force of Chile to carry out their fundamental obligation and save the integrity of our nation.

On September 11 we acted, driven only by the oath we took many years ago, to defend our country and combine our efforts to preserve Chile as a sovereign nation, prosperous and free. We acted in concordance with the immense majority of our countrymen, who, in fear and desperation, saw how an ideology alien to our history was taking advantage cleverly of our judicial structure in order to impose upon us a totalitarian regime. We acted as institutions, without the influence of any leader. The government junta that currently presides over Chile, with the support of the nation, is made up of men who do not seek power and who lack personal ambition. They are only a single body, patriotically united, that has taken on the immense but inevitable responsibility of restoring our homeland.

I must draw the attention of the representatives to the agreement adopted by the joint session of the Supreme Court of Justice two days later, on September 13. Through this agreement, the highest court of the Republic, recognizing the intention of the new government to respect and implement the decisions of the judiciary, without a prior administrative examination of its legality, ordered the nation's courts to continue their work, certain that the administrative authority would guarantee the normal discharge of its obligations.

The present government has sought and immediately received the patriotic cooperation of professional people, technicians, workers, employees, businessmen and craftsmen. The government has emphasized that its basic purpose will be the implementation of effective social justice, which will never be achieved through deceit, easy promises, bribery or the criminal division of our people. Rather, it will be done through honest work, a common dedication and community of interest. The present government is not the return to a recent or remote past. The workers have fought far too long and far too hard defending their legitimate rights for that. The armed forces are a part of this noble people and we shall never betray those who, like ourselves, have dedicated their efforts to return Chile to the place history has reserved for it.

We maintain our traditional respect for and hospitality to foreigners; but we shall be very careful to avoid a repetition of the reprehensible acts of foreign intervention that have caused the country so much suffering. With the assistance of everyone, we shall rebuild Chile.

The armed forces and the police force have assumed the task of redirecting the country along the path of liberty and law. Once we have achieved our goal, we shall not hesitate to withdraw to our barracks and to our ships. The time needed to return to normalcy will be as brief as possible and will depend to a large extent upon the efforts of all Chileans dedicated to that noble end.

A guiding principle of our foreign policy will be the usual principle of non-intervention in the domestic or external affairs of other states. But as we solemnly promised to respect national sovereignty, and therefore its obvious corollary, the self-determination of peoples, so must I categorically declare that we shall never allow foreign intrusion in our internal affairs or in the conduct of our international policy. To comply with this fundamental principle, one of our first acts was to sever diplomatic and consular relations with the present government of Cuba. We have been able to prove that over the last years there has been constant infiltration of Cuban agents, some official and some unofficial, in our internal politics and even in our foreign policy. When the break came, 42 Cuban diplomatic officials were accredited to Chile, as opposed to six Chileans in Havana, and of those only two belonged to the foreign service. Last September, 987 Castro Cubans were discovered to be illegal residents of my country. In the course of the present year, from 1 January to 31 July, 633 people came to Chile from Havana on diplomatic or official business. They intervened in every political, economic and functional organization of the state and, above all, in the very presidency of the Republic. Instructors and top leaders of the paramilitary groups were either Cuban or had been trained by Cubans.

It has been fully proved that gun-running was an institution of the government, protected by the government. Thus, for example, in March of last year, 13 cases were known to have arrived in Chile, flown in on a regular Cuban airline flight and intended for the purpose of the presidency of the Republic. Those cases did not go through regular customs, but were received directly by the Chief of the Chilean Political Police. When the Chamber of Deputies duly protested, the then authorities maintained that the cases contained "works of art sent as gifts by Premier Fidel Castro." Now we have become more familiar with the characteristics of those "works of art"; 13 cases contained 472 side arms and machine-guns, two sub-machine-guns and 40,000 cartridges.

The weapons and ammunition thus far found in the hands of the misnamed "popular militia" are not the type used by the Chilean armed forces, and their amount is really surprising. They included not only side arms and submachine-guns, but also heavy machine-guns, rocket launchers, antitank guns, 106mm cannons as well as enormous amounts of explosives. This arsenal, brought into Chile principally from Cuba through the surreptitious procedures I have described, was mainly manufactured in the Soviet Union and Czechoslovakia. According to what has been thus far discovered, it would be enough to equip an army of 20,000 men.

I do not wish to go into the details of this Cuban infiltration in Chilean internal affairs. But I should like to read out a hand-written letter from Premier Fidel Castro to the President of Chile, dated 29 July, 1973. In order better to understand its terms, I must recall that a short time before, in circumstances that are still mysterious, the distinguished Aide de Camp of the Chief of State, Commander Araya, had been assassinated. The reaction of that new political crime was so great in Chile that the Chief of State instituted a dialogue with the chief opposition party, the Christian Democrats. That dialogue turned out to be hopeless because the President's obvious desire was to gain time without offering any concrete solution to the problems. At that moment, Cuban Minister Carlos Rafael Rodrigues and Chief of Secret Police Manuel Pineiro chose to arrive in Santiago, ostensibly to discuss the conference of non-aligned countries. They carried with them the hand-written letter from Premier Castro. I have a photostat of it in my hand and any representative who may wish to read it can ask for a copy from the Chilean delegation. I shall read out the contents of the letter; it is extremely important because of its implications. It reads as follows:

Havana, 29 July 1973.

Dear Salvador:

Under the pretext of discussing with you question. concerning the meeting on non-aligned countries, Carlos and Pineiro have gone to see you. The real purpose is to discuss with you your situation and, as always, to offer you our willingness to cooperate in the face of the difficulties and dangers which hinder and threaten the process. Their stay will be very short, since they have many pending obligations here, and it is not without sacrifice to their work that we decided that the trip should be made.

I see that you are now taken up in the delicate question of the dialogue with the Christian Democrats in a serious atmosphere created by the brutal assassination of your Naval Aide de Camp and of the new truck owners strike. I can therefore quite well imagine the great tension that exists and your desire to gain time to improve the relationship of forces in case a battle breaks out and, if possible, to find a way to allow the revolutionary process to continue without civil strife, while protecting your historic responsibility for what might occur. These are laudable goals. But if the other side, whose real intentions we are not in a position to evaluate from here, should insist upon a treacherous and irresponsible policy that would exact an impossible price from Unidad Popular and the revolution, which is in itself quite likely, do not for one minute forget the formidable strength of the Chilean working classes and the strong support they have always offered you in your difficult moments. If you should call upon them because the revolution is in danger, they can paralyze those that threaten to overthrow the government, preserve the loyalty of those who hesitate, and impose their conditions and decide once and for all, if necessary, on the future of Chile. The enemy should know that the working class is forewarned and ready for action. Their force and combativeness can tip the balance in the capital in your favour, even though other circumstances might be unfavourable.

Your determination to defend the process strongly and

with the greatest honour possible, even if it means risking your own life, will draw to your side all the forces able to fight and the worthwhile men and women in Chile. Your courage, your serenity and your daring in this historic moment of your country and, above all, your strong resolve and heroic leadership, hold the key to the situation.

Let Carlos and Manuel know how your loyal Cuban friends can help you.

Once again I send you the affection and unlimited confidence of the Cuban people.

Fraternally,
Fidel Castro

On the basis of the fact that we can maintain normal relations only with those countries which respect us, we also severed relations with the People's and Democratic Republic of Korea—after we were able to prove that there had been intervention in our internal affairs and an involvement of that country's diplomatic representatives in the training of guerrillas in Chile.

On the other hand, we wish to maintain diplomatic relations with all countries of the world, irrespective of their ideology, political, social or economic systems. We believe that the diversity of governments has nothing whatever to do with relations among states. Ideological pluralism is and will be another element of our foreign policy. For these reasons we regret that certain governments to which we had expressed Chile's desire to maintain relations on a normal basis have nevertheless decided to break off such relations with a curious uniformity and under the most varied and false pretences.

Within the strange tangle of falsehoods that have been spread abroad as a result of the events of 11 September, news has been circulated that Chile would return all refugees from political, racial or religious persecution to their countries of origin. From the very outset I have re-assured the Secretary-General of the United Nations—and I do so again from this rostrum—that such refugees who are in Chile legally and have not been implicated in any crime are fully protected, but others who are expelled will not be returned to their countries of origin but will be allowed to choose their destination. After very pleasant discussions with the Regional Representative for Latin America of the United Nations High Commissioner for Refugees we have reached a general and mutually satisfactory agreement. We stated that we will accept his help when it comes to practical solutions that might affect refugees who have decided to seek Chilean hospitality.

I understand fully the interest that these events have aroused in the world, even in countries very distant from my own, countries which are relatively unfamiliar with our idiosyncracies, our traditions, and the vigour of our people. There is no doubt that the so-called "Chilean experience" of a transition toward socialism, aroused the curiosity and perhaps even the sympathy and warmth of many countries who saw in this example of the so-called Popular Unity, a path worthy of imitation or at least of assimilation. But it is one thing to assess a foreign experience from afar, seated in comfortable armchairs or in discussion around a well-served table, and it is quite another thing to experience it.

Contrary to what the Chilean people themselves believed at first, it was no evolution or social progress that was taking place in Chile. There was simply a power machine being set up by which, through the use of legal loopholes at first, and later through open and outright illegality, the country was being led to tyranny and consolidated totalitarianism.

The Chilean people did not deserve to pay such a "high cost of revolution," as some came to call the loss of lives, suffering, discrimination, hunger and sectarianism brought about by the Unidad Popular. Worse still, my country, on the border of financial and economic bankruptcy, plagued by misery and divided into irreconcilable camps, was on the verge of falling into complete chaos and into a dissolution of the very essence of the nation. In a supreme effort, and after having exhausted every legal possibility, my country has been able to avoid the most cruel and brutal of civil wars and set its feet on the road to national reconstruction.

None of this could escape the uncommitted foreigners who live in Chile, and much less the diplomatic representatives of friendly nations who looked on impartially but with agony, while the country disintegrated. Politicians and ideologists outside the country must have had another view. I remind them of the words of Bossuet: "The worst aberration of the mind consists of seeing things as one would like them to be and not as they are."

Chile has now taken a different road. The new government will not retreat by one step from the victories won by the workers, or from its policy of absolute national independence. We will wholeheartedly defend the interests of Chile in the face of any kind of imperialism.

Plotting the Coup

JONATHAN KANDELL

This article appeared in the New York Times *issue of September 27, 1973 under the title "Chilean Officers Tell How They Began to Plan the Take-Over Last November."*

Middle-ranking officers of all three military services began plotting the coup against President Salvador Allende Gossens as far back as November, 1972, conversations with officers and civilians close to the situation have revealed.

The officers planning the coup, which resulted in the death of President Allende on Sept. 11, held discussions with one another and with middle-class union and business leaders.

By August of this year, the military leaders had rejected any thought of a civilian political solution and had encouraged middle-class unions to continue their prolonged strikes against Dr. Allende's government to set the stage for a military take-over.

"We would have acted even if Allende had called a plebiscite or reached a compromise with the political opposition," said an officer deeply involved in the plotting of the coup.

Although the actual order for the coup was given on the afternoon of Sept. 10, military garrisons throughout the country had been put on the alert about ten days earlier.

To make certain that there were no breakdowns, officers considered loyal to the Allende government were placed under arrest when the take-over began. In some cases junior officers arrested their commanders.

Most Were Anti-Marxist

The details of the military coup were given and cross-checked in separate conversations with officers of all three military branches and with civilians who had kept themselves closely informed of developments as the coup was being hatched. The informants asked that their names not be revealed or their service branches cited. The vast majority of the officers of the Chilean armed forces were staunch anti-Marxists even before Dr. Allende assumed the presidency in November, 1970.

"After Allende came in, we believed that he deliberately set about to destroy this country's institutions," one officer said. "In the first two years, he had succeeded in destroying the economic power of the middle-class, which is the base of our national institutions. At the same time, all political parties suffered a tremendous decline in prestige because of their ineffectiveness" in halting Dr. Allende's socialization programs.

Other officers asserted that they were further motivated by what they interpreted as an attempt by the government to plan on natural rivalries between the military branches and prevent the formation of a common front.

"Under Allende, the defense ministers actively fostered competition between the services in fund allocations," said an officer. "Some of the examples may sound petty, but taken together there was a pattern."

Raise, Then Runaround

"Sometimes," he continued, "the naval air force was favored over the air force in equipment purchases and sometimes it was the other way around. At one point, Allende's defense minister granted a 25 per cent pay increase to air force pilots, and then turned around and encouraged the army to oppose it."

But these officers asserted that the first attempts to coordinate action in the army, navy and air force against the Allende government grew out of a 26-day general strike of business and transportation in October, 1972. The strike ended when Dr. Allende invited Gen. Carlos Prats Gonzalez, the army's Commander in Chief, and two other officers into the Cabinet.

"Just about everybody in the armed forces welcomed this," an officer said, "because at the time we considered Prats a traditional military man who would put a brake on Allende."

But almost immediately, General Prats came to be viewed as favorable to the Allende government. By late November, army and air force colonels and navy commanders began to map out the possibilities of a coup. They also contacted leaders of the truck owners, shopkeepers and professional associations, as well as key businessmen, who had backed the October strike.

"We left the generals and admirals out of the plotting," an officer said, "because we felt that some of them like Prats would refuse to go along."

Pause for an Election

The greatest obstacle, according to these officers, was the armed forces' 40-year tradition of political neutrality: "I could have pulled my hair out for teaching my students for all those years that the armed forces must never rebel against the constitutional government," said an officer who formerly taught history at a military academy. "It took a long time to convince officers that there was no other way out."

The plotting subsided somewhat in the weeks of political campaigning leading to the March legislative elections. The civilian opposition to Dr. Allende thought it could emerge with two-thirds of the legislative seats and thus impeach the President.

"It was supposed to be a last chance for a political solution," one officer admitted. "But frankly, many of us gave a sigh of relief when the Marxists received such a high vote because we felt that no politician could run the country and that eventually the Marxists might be even stronger." The Marxists' vote was 43 per cent.

By the middle of March, the plotting resumed and colonels involved invited a number of generals and admirals to join. "In April, the government somehow found out that we were plotting," said an officer, "and they started to consider ways of stopping us."

All the officers interviewed asserted that the Allende government began secretly to stockpile weapons and train paramilitary forces in factories and rural areas with the intention of assassinating key military leaders and carrying out a "countercoup."

3 Touchy Episodes

The military informants said there were three episodes before the Sept. 11 coup that could have led to an unplanned, bloody military revolt and possibly civil war.

64   On May 18, the commander of an air force base in Santiago threatened to carry out his own coup. But it was discovered by a pro-Allende colonel who commanded a neighboring infantry regiment, and who threatened to attack the air base.

The most publicized was the abortive coup of June 29, in which about 100 members of an armored regiment in Santiago, led by Lieut. Col. Roberto Souper, took part.

On Aug. 18, President Allende and, allegedly, General Prats, forced the resignation of Gen. Cesar Ruiz Danyou, the air force commander in chief. Jets streaked out of Santiago to the southern city of Concepcion to prepare for an immediate coup. But leaders of all three branches urged their officers to wait until General Prats could be removed; General Ruiz also pleaded with his men to abandon the idea of immediate action.

The leaders of the three branches then confronted General Prats and demanded his immediate resignation.

As soon as General Prats resigned, on Aug. 23, along with two other generals considered to be pro-Allende, the high command of all three service branches began mapping out the details of their take-over.

The stage had already been set by the strike of 40,000 truck owners, joined by hundreds of thousands of professional employees, shopkeepers and small businessmen.

The military had also embarked on an intense campaign of arms searches in leftist strongholds, and used these searches as an excuse virtually to control road transit in and out of major cities.

The military leaders had told President Allende two weeks before the coup that they would not act if he could settle the strikes and reach a political compromise with the Christian Democrats—the largest political opposition party.

The Final Touches

In fact, the military informants asserted, nothing could have stopped the coup, once General Prats resigned. "We were only putting the final touches on the plan," one officer said.

On Sept. 1, military garrisons throughout the country were put on the alert. When the final order was given on the afternoon of Sept. 10, about 50 officers suspected of being for Dr. Allende were arrested. Most are still detained, including at least three generals and one admiral.

Early in the morning of Sept. 11, troops throughout the country seized all radio and television stations, attacked leftist party headquarters and rounded up thousands of leading Marxists.

Like the military junta, the middle-ranking officers interviewed denied that President Allende was killed, insisting that he had committed suicide rather than surrender. General Prats was allowed to leave the country, but only after he appeared on national television a few days after the coup to deny news reports that he was leading an insurgent army south of Santiago.

Manchester Guardian, October 6, 1973: Chile's Incipient Fascism

RICHARD GOTT

With each day that passes it becomes increasingly clear that the military coup in Chile has unleashed forces that the military junta is unable to control. By destroying the organized left—its political parties, its newspapers, and its trade union movement—the balance of forces has swung dramatically to the right, further even than some senior members of the armed forces had contemplated, certainly further than the Christian Democrat Party desired.

The entire power of the state, which before has served to protect if not actually to assist the organizations of the extreme left, has now fallen in behind the extremist groups on the right which are now able to operate with impunity.

While the military junta itself attempts to maintain a Boy Scout image of healthy clean-living generals who have rescued the country from bankruptcy, chaos, and civil war, the organized right-wing is proceeding apace with its plans to liquidate its opponents and to ensure that the left in Chile never has a chance to return to power.

In a country as open and democratic as Chile, no one hides his political feelings. Throughout the country, in every large town or small community, the political militants are known. Consequently, no one feels safe. Anyone who has ever opened his mouth to speak up in favour of socialism, whether on the factory floor, university lecture room, or peasants council, finds himself a possible target for denunciation.

For many people this means a visit from the police, a trip to the police station, and a subsequent journey to the cells of the National Stadium, the holds of the steamship *Lebu*, or a voyage to Dawson Island or Pisagua. Possibly they are the lucky ones. For in the shanty towns and out in the countryside there seems to be more summary justice.

As the prospect of civil war fades away, and the fact is that Chile has experienced a relatively tranquil change of government (5,000 dead in the first week still seems a large estimate), there is also the fact that people are still being killed. Quite apart from the half dozen reported cases of people being brought before military tribunals and then shot, there are the continuing raids by the military in the shanty towns which all seem to produce their sad little processions at the cemetery the next morning.

Little can be proved. One can only sift the rumors, observe the faces of the shanty town dwellers as they stonily deny that anything untoward has happened, talk to people released from detention, and draw one's conclusions. Chile, even after three years travel along the road to socialism, is still as desperately divided socially and economically as the countries of Southern Africa.

The visiting journalist, whatever his prejudices, inevitably falls among the middle class, and that class has no more contact with the life of the Chilean "roto" than the white burghers of Johannesburg have with the black inhabitants of the township of Soweto.

But even the most conservative Chilean seems to have a wayward child who has joined the Socialist Party, or whose daughter has married into the MIR. Perhaps most important of all, they all have a maid. She may live in a poky bedroom at the back of the house, but her sisters and her cousins and her aunts live in the shanty towns and have eyes to see. Consequently, almost everyone has an inkling of what is going on, and many people are desperately afraid. Nor is there any way of alleviating their fear.

The military is a law unto itself, and because of its very unfamiliarity with the techniques of open political intervention, it behaves more brusquely than other Latin American armies might do in comparable circumstances. With tens of thousands detained throughout the country, with permanent military raids, not just in the shanty towns but in the most respectable areas of the city, the Chileans find themselves in as novel a situation as would an Englishman if this routine had become the norm of life in London.

The Chilean soldiers, having no experience in these matters, can behave with conspicuous brutality. The junta's ambition is to impose order and to finish with chaos and anarchy, but in the process their soldiery inevitably sows fresh seeds of disorder. The tales of rape and robbery that accompany the searches for arms are legion. Secondly, in its enthusiasm for abolishing politics, the military have inevitably had recourse to that political group which represents the most conservative sector in Chilean society.

This sector, of course, thinks that it has no politics, and believes that it upholds the eternal interests of the Chilean nation, manifested in the institutions that it has inherited from a previous century. But this group, represented by the National Party, has no positive ideology. It harks back to a previous era, before that of Allende, before that of Eduardo Frei, back to an imagined golden age when students, peasants, and workers knew their place and took their orders from a class that was born to rule. The prospect in 1973 of reviving a particular view of Chile that existed ten or 20 years ago is exceedingly dim. The country has changed too much.

An interesting example of the rejection of conservatism is the case of the "Jornada Unica." In the old days, importing a Mediterranean habit, all Chile took a siesta in the afternoon. President Frei, with much enthusiasm for efficiency and modernity, abolished the siesta, and sensibly ordained an unbroken workday—the "Jornada Unica." One of the first acts of the junta was to reinstate the siesta, since its abolition had met with bitter resistance. But by now the shopkeepers have become used to their new work schedule and are reluctant to climb into a bus four times a day. They are now protesting against the junta's new regulations.

Into the ideological vacuum created by the collapse of the left and the utopian conservatism of the junta neatly falls the fascist movement "Fatherland and Freedom." When last heard of, this movement was supporting the failed military coup on June 29. Subsequently its leaders disappeared into clandestinity or into exile. Then shortly before the coup on September 11, its secretary, General Roberto Theiem, was captured in a suburban restaurant, and its founder, Pablo Rodriguez, appeared in Temuco. Last Friday both reappeared in a Santiago hotel.

Theiem is a crewcut Teuton and looks like an astronaut. Rodriguez is a Chilean lawyer, immensely articulate. Unlike the junta, who propose national renovation, Rodriguez wants a nationalist revolution. He claims that the institutions of Chilean society are out of date and collapsing. They need to be replaced rather than shored up.

In spite of his emphasis on Chilean nationalism, Rodriguez is recognizably a fascist in a familiar European mold. He uses words like "integral" and "corporative" without batting an eyelid. "We realized that Marxism-Leninism could not be fought just with anti-Marxism," he said. "It had to be opposed with an idea—that of a nationalist revolution."

The "Fatherland and Freedom" organization has now dissolved itself. It supports the junta, but believes that the task of the government is to undertake "the transformation of all the institutions in Chile." So far that is not the wish of the government, which wants to preserve not to transform.

But, as this becomes seen to be a hopeless task, the arguments of these right wing extremists in favor of a fascist revolution will surely grow. For more than a decade the vast majority of Chileans have voted for a change—Christians and Marxists have been given their chance. Now, waiting in the wings—and undoubtedly strong within the armed forces—the fascists may be about to be given their turn.

Luis Ramallo's Visit to the Santiago Morgue, September 19, 1973

The following cable to UNESCO/Paris was sent on October 5, 1973 from Santiago by Mr. Ramallo. who at the time was acting Secretary-General of the Latin American Faculty of the Social Sciences (FLACSO)

OPERATOR FOR ONWARD IMMEDIATE CONFIDENTIAL RETRANSMISSION TO DESTINATION: UNESCO: PARIS

URGENT FOR YOUR POSSIBLE ACTION FLACSO DIRECTIVE COMMITTEE INFORMS YOU OF EXTREMELY GRAVE CIRCUMSTANCES INVOLVING THE DEATH OF TWO FLACSO STUDENTS FROM BOLIVIA WHILE THEY WERE UNDER THE CUSTODY OF CHILEAN MILITARY AUTHORITIES SUBJECT TO INTERROGATION THE NATURE OF WHICH WE ARE NOT AWARE

OF AND WITHOUT ANY OFFICIAL COM-
MUNICATION TO FLACSO EITHER PRIOR OR
SUBSEQUENT TO THEIR DEATHS STOP
FOLLOWING ARE ESSENTIAL DETAILS
PRIMO JORGE RIOS DALENZ *AAA* TAKEN
BY MILITARY PATROL FROM HIS PERMANENT
DOMICILE IN THE PRESENCE OF WIFE AND TWO
CHILDREN AGES NINE AND EIGHT ON SEP-
TEMBER TWELVE *BBB* DOMICILE REVISITED
AFTERWARDS BY MILITARY ON TWO OC-
CASIONS WITH SUBTRACTIONS OF ALL PER-
SONAL IDENTIFICATION DOCUMENTS FROM
WIFE AND CHILDREN PLUS SOME BOOKS
REFLECTING MARXIST IDEOLOGY *CCC* RIOS
WAS SEEN ON MULTIPLE OCCASIONS BY
SEVERAL WITNESSES UNTIL EVENING SEP-
TEMBER FOURTEEN INSIDE OF DETENTION
CENTER BEING INTERROGATED UNDER OWN
NAME *DDD* ON SEPTEMBER NINETEEN
ACTING UPON AN ANONYMOUS TELEPHONE
CALL BOTH HIS WIFE AND MYSELF PER-
SONALLY RECOGNIZED HIS UNIDENTIFIED
BULLET RIDDEN BODY WITH SIGNS OF
MULTIPLE CONCUSSIONS AND TWO
LARGE GAPING WOUNDS IN CHEST AND LEGS
BODY WAS FOUND AMONG SOME ONE HUN-
DRED FIFTY SIMILARLY UNIDENTIFIED AND
WOUNDED BODIES IN THE PUBLIC MORTUARY
WHERE IT HAD BEEN DEPOSITED BY
MILITARY *EEE* FAMILY WAS LATER
REPATRIATED TO BOLIVIA TAKING WITH
THEM CREMATED REMAINS RIOS *FFF* MY
STRONG VERBAL PROTEST FOLLOWED BY
WRITTEN ONE TO FOREIGN AFFAIRS UN-
DERSECRETARY HAS RECEIVED AS YET NO
OFFICIAL REPLY BUT UNOFFICIAL REPORT
GIVEN BY HIM VERBALLY IS THAT RIOS WOULD
APPEAR TO HAVE BEEN KILLED WHILE AT-
TEMPTING ESCAPE STOP SECUNDO IGNACIO
SOTO QUIROGA ALSO FROM BOLIVIA
AAA TAKEN TOGETHER WITH WIFE AND
A FAMILY FRIEND FROM HIS DOMICILE IN
THE PRESENCE OF HIS MOTHER ON SEP-
TEMBER TWENTY SIXTH AND DRIVEN TO A

72   SPECIAL INTERROGATION CENTER OF
MILITARY INTELLIGENCE *BBB* WIFE LATER
APPEARED AT THE GENERAL DETENTION CAMP
FROM WHERE WE HAVE BEEN VERBALLY
NOTIFIED THAT SHE SHALL BE ENTRUSTED
TO US TODAY FOR IMMEDIATE RE-
PATRIATION *CCC* ON OCTOBER FIRST
WHILE INQUIRING ROUTINELY FROM
DETENTION CENTER AUTHORITIES ABOUT
OTHER MEMBERS OF INTERNATIONAL COM-
MUNITY UNDER DETENTION I WAS INFORMED
THAT SOTO HAD DIED WHEN IN THE MIDDLE
OF AN INTERROGATION HE HAD PLUNGED OUT
OF A THIRD FLOOR WINDOW *DDD* LATER
THAT SAME DAY HIS BROTHER INFORMED ME
THAT ON SEPTEMBER TWENTY NINTH AND
ACTING UPON A PRIVATE TIP HE AND HIS
MOTHER HAD IN FACT CLAIMED AND BURIED
THE BODY OF IGNACIO SOTO WHICH HAD BEEN
DEPOSITED AND PROPERLY IDENTIFIED BY
THE SAME MILITARY GROUP AS JORGE RIOS
AND LISTED AS A SUICIDE TERTIO FLACSO
DIRECTIVE COMMITTEE AND MYSELF PER-
SONALLY WANT YOU TO KNOW THAT BOTH
VICTIMS WERE AMONG OUR BEST MOST
CONSCIENTIOUS STUDENTS AND THAT WE
ABSOLUTELY BELIEVE FOR MULTIPLE
REASONS THAT THEY NEVER ACTED IN ANY
WAY AS TO INTERFERE IN MATTERS OF
CHILEAN SECURITY NOT EVEN IN LOCAL
POLITICAL ACTIVITY QUARTO IN VIEW OF
THESE FACTS WHICH HAVE CAUSED FLACSO
AND LOCAL INTERNATIONAL COMMUNITY A
SENSE OF HORROR AND OUTRAGE WE HAVE
TAKEN FOLLOWING ACTION *AAA* WE SENT
VERY STRONGLY WORDED PROTESTS TO CHILE
FOREIGN MINISTER COPY OF WHICH ARE
BEING FORWARDED TO YOU THIS WEEK
POUCH *BBB* WE BROUGHT TO A HALT THE
ACADEMIC ACTIVITIES RELATED TO THE
PRESENT PROMOTION OF THE TWO FLACSO
SCHOOLS AS OF OCTOBER FIRST AND ORDERED
THE IMMEDIATE REPATRIATION OF ALL OUR
NON CHILEAN STUDENTS AS A SIGN OF OUR

PROTEST AND DISHEARTENMENT FOR LACK OF ADEQUATE HUMAN GUARANTEES FOR OUR STUDENTS ON THE PART OF HOST COUNTRY *CCC* WE CONTINUE RESEARCH ACTIVITIES AS USUAL, ALSO HAVE TAKEN ADEQUATE MEASURES FOR PROVIDING REPATRIATED STUDENTS WITH ACADEMIC DIRECTION IN THE FINALIZING OF THEIR MASTER'S DEGREE DISSERTATIONS DURING THE REMAINING THREE MONTHS OF THEIR ACADEMIC YEAR IN THEIR RESPECTIVE COUNTRIES SO AS TO ASSURE THEIR PROPER GRADUATION QUINTO WHILE THERE IS AN IMPROVEMENT IN THE EFFORTS BY NEW AUTHORITIES TO SAFEGUARD THE PREMISES AND THE INTERNATIONAL STAFF OF FLACSO NEVERTHELESS RESPONSIBILITIES IN THE CASE OF STUDENTS AND LOCAL PERSONNEL ARE NOT DISCHARGED AS THE FACTS HERE RELATED SHOW STOP FLACSO ASKS THAT IN THE NAME OF FUNDAMENTAL PRINCIPLES OF UNITED NATIONS AND IN THE CONTEXT OF PRESUMED VIOLATIONS OF HUMAN RIGHTS OF FOREIGNERS LIVING IN CHILE ALL PRESSURE BE BROUGHT ON THE HOLDERS OF MILITARY POWER TO OBTAIN AN ADEQUATE HUMAN TREATMENT WHILE THEY ARE DEFENSELESS IN THE HANDS OF MILITARY FOR FOLLOWING MEMBERS OF FLACSO COMMUNITY NAMELY JORGE KLEIN A FRENCH CHILEAN ROBERTO METZGER A BRAZILIAN LUIS ALBERTO ALFONSO A COLUMBIAN EDEN OLIVEIRA A URUGUAYAN LUIS CIFUENTES AND JUAN VILLALOBOS CHILEANS SEXTO FINALLY WE WANT YOU TO KNOW THAT AT THIS SORROWFUL TIME WE HAVE BEEN COMFORTED BY THE GREAT SOLIDARITY SHOWN TO US BY LOCAL UNITED NATIONS FAMILY OFFICIALS AS WELL AS BY THE DEEP SENSE IN OUR WHOLE FLACSO COMMUNITY OF THE FUNDAMENTAL CORRECTNESS OF OUR ATTITUDE IN THE PAST AS WELL AS AT THIS TIME AND BY THE EXCEPTIONAL MEMORY OF OUR TWO STUDENTS SO VIOLENTLY AND SEN-

74   SELESSLY TAKEN AWAY FROM US AND FROM
THE FUTURE OF THE BOLIVIAN NATION

RAMALLO

THE POLITICAL PEOPLE RESPOND

The first document in this section was circulated almost immediately after the coup and made its way out of Chile via Argentina. It is representative of an important, although minority, sentiment within the reformist Christian Democratic Party, the nation's major political grouping. It was this faction which earlier had favored a dialogue with the Allende government and the possibility of joining it if sufficient concessions were made. Next we have the official statement of the Christian Democratic Party, also known as the Frei faction, after ex-President Eduardo Frei. Almost immediately after the coup, the governing council of the Party and some of its major personalities, including Frei, gave approval to the coup. Since then all political parties have been suspended, and the Marxist ones outlawed. The clandestine statement of the Communist Party of Chile is made in this spirit. Next appears another clandestine document, the results of an interview with Miguel Enriquez, leader of the extreme-leftist movement MIR. Now in hiding, he, among other things, gently criticizes the Allende government for not being brusque enough with the opposition when it was in power. The last document features an interview with

76 *Senator Francisco Bulnes, a conservative leader who is a symbol of the traditional upper-class values of the nation. It is interesting that even he strains for Chile to return to a constitutional process of sorts. It might be added that the ruling junta is on record as scorning the political parties of all persuasions as well as the parliamentary process.*

Dissenting Christian Democratic Voices

The following statement was issued on September 13, 1973 and was obtained through Chilean intermediaries. It was signed by 12 members of the left wing faction of the Christian Democratic Party including such notables as Senator Renan Fuentealba and Congressman Bernardo Leighton.

Today, the 13th of September 1973, the undersigned, attesting that this is the first occasion on which we have been able to come together to concord our judgments and express our position after the completion of the military coup of the day before yesterday, make the following declaration:

1. We categorically condemn the overthrow of the Constitutional President of Chile, Mr. Salvador Allende, whose government, in accordance with the popular will of our Party, we unwaveringly opposed. We bow respectfully before the sacrifice which he made of his life in defense of Constitutional authority.

2. We wish to clarify that our opposition to his government was always based on the intention of preserving the continuity of the process of change which the government of the Christian Democrats had the honor to begin in our country and at the same time to restrain it from antidemocratic deviation.

We maintain in their entirety those criticisms which we expressed in this context concerning the government of Popular Unity and of President Allende. We repeat, moreover, that, in conformity with our personal convictions and with the often expressed intentions of the Christian Democrats, we never took any other position in parliament or elsewhere that was not opposition within the democratic process intended to obtain the correction of the errors committed by the government of President Allende which we resisted.

3. The failure to make these corrections, which finally led to the tragedy, is the responsibility of all, both government and opposition, because the duty of maintaining a democracy cannot be avoided by anyone. But in our judgment there were those who had greater responsibility for what occurred. In the first place, there was the sectarian dogmatism of the Popular Unity, which was not able to build an authentically democratic path to socialism adapted to our national character. Special condemnation is deserved for the irresponsibility of the far left.

In the second place, the economic right wing, which, with cold determination took advantage of the errors of the Popular Unity to create a climate of tension, blindness and political passion, united to the above, made impossible even a minimum of consensus, discrediting those who sought it with objectivity and good judgment.

4. These extreme sectors psychologically alienated public opinion and, in conjunction with many political and military people, created the false impression that there was no other solution to the crisis of Chile than armed confrontation or a coup d'etat.

We reiterate today, as always, our profound conviction that, within the democratic process, we could have avoided the installation in Chile of a totalitarian regime, without the necessity of paying the cost in human life and the inevitable excesses produced by solutions imposed by force.

5. The military junta has expressed its intention of returning power to the will of the people and of respecting its public liberties. We welcome this intention as positive for the restoration of democracy and of social peace, and we hope it will be accomplished without delay in accordance with their expressed declarations.

6. As for ourselves, we believe that our supreme responsibility in this hour, which we assume above all other considerations, resides in continuing the struggle for the principles of Christian Democracy and for the restoration of Chilean democracy.

The facts that we deplore today indicate that only in liberty supported by the majority of the people, and not by exclusionary minorities, can be realized the humanistic and democratic transformation of Chile which constitutes our goal and strengthens our will.

The Christian Democratic Evaluation of Chile Under the Junta and the Future of National Institutions

The following is the official statement of the governing council of the Christian Democratic Party (C.D.P.) which was issued on September 27, 1973.

In order to orient its militants and sympathizers and —as fully as is possible—public opinion; to give its frank, disinterested and patriotic opinion to those who have taken over the government and to establish for the historical record the responsibility of each person, the National Council of the Christian Democratic Party believes it is necessary to clarify its judgment and attitude with respect to the grave and abnormal situation which exists in the Republic.

In the present document will be covered, successively, the following points:

a. the events which led to the change of government;

b. the opinion of the C.D.P. with respect to these events;

c. the characteristics of the current situation and the prospects which it represents for the nation, and

d. the position of the C.D.P. with regard to these new conditions.

I. The Violent Change of Government

1. On the 11th of September of this year the armed forces and the Carabineros (para-military police) over-threw the government presided over by Salvador Allende and assumed power in his stead, establishing a ruling military junta.

2. The confrontation caused by this action produced many casualties, among them that of the President of the Republic himself, who committed suicide in the La Moneda Palace. The palace was bombarded and was largely destroyed. The precise number of dead and wounded is not known; however, it is certainly considerable. There are major material damages. The military actions undertaken to uncover and snuff out certain pockets of resistance, to arrest armed groups and individuals and to prevent future acts of sabotage have continued for several days.

3. The development of events revealed the existence of an enormous quantity of armaments and explosives in the hands of the parties, groups, and persons associated with the overthrown government, which came to constitute a veritable parallel army. It also came to light that thousands of foreigners, many of them protected by diplomatic missions of socialist countries, acted as instructors or active members of these illegal armed forces. All of this supports the assumption that the so-called Popular Unity, consisting fundamentally of the Communist and Socialist Parties, was preparing to take complete power by means of an armed coup.

4. The armed forces and the Carabineros have justified their action by calling attention, in Proclamation No. 5 of the ruling military junta, to the numerous abuses committed by the previous government, which may be summarized as follows:

   a. decay of the basic rights of freedom of expression and of instruction, of association, of petition, of the right to strike, of the rights of

property and, in general, the right to a dignified life
and security of subsistence;

b. destruction of national unity, artificial
fomenting of class warfare, the loss of the contribution of Chileans to the good of the nation and
the unleashing of a blind and fratricidal war
behind strange, false, and fallacious ideas;

c. inability to maintain the possibility for Chileans
to live side by side together, due to lack of respect
or compliance with the law which was gravely
damaged;

d. flagrant and repeated violation of the Constitution by means of questionable judgments and
twisted interpretations;

e. flouting of the laws, by means of the subterfuge
of "legal loopholes;"

f. loss of the mutual respect which the Powers of
the State must have for each other, which rendered
ineffective the decisions of the National Congress,
of the Judiciary, and of the office of the Comptroller-General of the Republic, with inadmissible
excuses or simply without explanation;

g. excesses on the part of the Executive branch
beyond its mandate in taking into its own hands the
bulk of political and economic power with con-
sequent grave danger to all the rights and liberties
of the citizenry;

h. subordination or capitulation of presidential
authority to the decisions of committees or
directives of political parties or groups;

i. stagnation or recession of the agricultural, industrial, and commercial economy of the country
and accelerated growth of inflation, and;

j. anarchy, stifling of liberties, moral and economic
degradation, irresponsibility and incompetence of

the government, which have worsened the situation of Chile;

5. On the basis of these reasons, the ruling military junta has expressed in several declarations that its purposes are to "struggle for the liberation of the Fatherland and prevent our country from falling under the Marxist yoke," to seek "the restoration of order and institutionality," to "reestablish the economic and social normality of the nation, peace, tranquility, and the security which were lost" and "the realization of an effective social justice" and that it was assuming power "only for as long as circumstances required, supported by the evidence of the feelings of the great majority of the nation."

II. Our Opinion with Regard to the Military Uprising

1. All of Chile knows that what occurred was not what the Christian Democratic Party struggled to obtain, because it is contrary to our democratic doctrine, our constitutionalist tradition, and our rejection of violence.

Faced by the fait accompli, the Party, respectful of the truth, admits that what occurred is primarily the consequence of the economic disaster, the institutional chaos, the armed violence and the profound moral crisis to which the deposed government led the nation. The incompetence, arbitrariness, the systematic scorn for the Constitution and the laws, the hateful sectarianism, the violence and corruption, which were characteristic signs of the governmental action of the so-called Popular Unity, came to gravely compromise the internal and external security of Chile and brought the majority of Chileans to anguish and despair.

It is necessary to point out that the blindness and passion with which certain reactionary sectors and damaged interests committed themselves to sharpening the conflict also contributed to provoking the situation, thus giving arguments and excuses for the action of the Marxist extremists.

The foregoing demonstrates that the government of Allende, motivated above all by the desire to take by any and all means the totality of power, had exhausted in the worst manner its so-called "Chilean way to socialism" and was preparing to stage a violent coup, which would have been terribly merciless and bloody, in order to install a communist dictatorship. Everything indicates that the armed forces did nothing more than to respond to this imminent risk. The foregoing explains the sensation of relief with which the majority of the citizens welcomed the military uprising.

2. The Party is conscious of having done, for its part, everything possible, even in the face of criticism and lack of comprehension, to preserve national unity, to keep the process of socio-economic changes within constitutional order, to obtain the correction of governmental abuses and its adherence to the law, to avoid hatred and violence, and to arrive, in short, at a democratic solution to the total crisis into which the nation had been plunged.

Expressive of the Party's conduct were such initiatives as the Constitutional Statute of Democratic Guarantees, intended to defend human rights in the face of the totalitarian menace; the law regarding arms control to avoid the risk of armed violence; the constitutional reform regarding the areas of the economy, for the purpose of regulating juridically the process of socialization and to establish the effective participation of the workers; the agrarian reform which established the compulsory allotment of land to the farmers in the areas of agrarian reform; various efforts directed toward the protection of the free expression of the freedom of the press and other media; and the mobilization of grass-roots organizations of workers, women, farmers, and students in defense of their fundamental rights.

Our constant struggle in parliament, in the media of mass communication, in the universities and throughout the social base of the nation, has been marked by the courage with which our leaders, militants, and sympathizers persevered, in the face of every sort of infamy, threats, and persecution. The blood of our comrades who fell victims of hatred in the struggle, is testimony to the resistance put up by the Party to the abuse and totalitarian spirit with which the Communist-Socialist government was destroying the nation's democratic unity. We never lost faith in our loyal commitment to save democracy in Chile and up to the final days of the deposed regime, we exhausted all our efforts to obtain from President Allende and his government the corrections which were indispensable to save the nation from institutional collapse and economic disaster. Lamentably, we failed, and were confronted by a wall of incomprehension, willful deceit, and intransigence.

3. Both the republican history of our nation and the institutional traditions of apoliticalism and pure professionalism of the armed forces and the Carabineros as well as its conduct with regard to President Allende, to whom they gave unrestricted obedience and with whose government they collaborated in ministerial and administrative functions, are sufficient proof that they believed that it was their unavoidable duty to save Chile from the imminent risk of civil war or a community tyranny.

These facts, and the trust which is owed to their honor as soldiers, lead one to believe that they will keep faith with their promise to establish a transitional, apolitical government, for the purpose of reestablishing the institutional, economic, and social normality of the country and that as soon as circumstances permit, they will return the power to the people so that it may independently decide its destiny by means of a secret and free election of the authorities who will govern them.

III. Characteristics and Perspectives of the Current Situation

1. Little more than 15 days after the change of government, the situation in the nation is tending toward normalization, though it is nevertheless far from being complete.

The whole territory of the nation finds itself under a state of siege, which as defined by the new authorities, signifies a "state of war" with its application of the norms of internal security and criminal law that operates by the military code.

Economic activities and those of public administration have resumed under the watchword that work and production are the great patriotic imperatives; the schools, however, have not yet reopened.

The supply of food and other essential goods has improved considerably, returning to the market and at lower prices, including basic necessities which had disappeared or could only be found on the black market.

2. The primary tasks of the military junta appear to be, up to now, the following:

> a. termination of the military mopping-up operation intended to expose and destroy every possible center of resistance, confiscation of the arms that they still have and apprehending the political, administrative, and union leaders of the previous regime;

> b. educating the public as to the economic destruction and the dangers to which the Marxist government led the country and the scandals caused by its personnel;

> c. eliminating every possibility of legitimate activity on the part of the Marxist sectors and eradicating "politics" from Chilean life, and;

> d. imposing order and discipline in work and in all national activities.

3. Many thousands of persons have been and continue to be deprived of their freedom and are being held in such places as the National Stadium in Santiago or certain regimental barracks. Their detention continues for many days, often without their families knowing where they are and without their being placed at the disposition of the judicial tribunals.

4. The ruling junta has closed the National Congress, has dissolved the Municipalities, has dissolved the Central Workers' Union and has declared the Marxist parties illegal. They have announced that the other parties shall be declared in recess. The publication of various newspapers and magazines has been suspended, as well as the broadcast of certain radio stations. A strict censorship has been imposed on the press, on radio, and on television. Certain universities have been taken over.

5. All the above clearly indicates that Chile is living under a dictatorial regime. The reasons which were given to justify the overthow of the previous regime in the military junta's Proclamation No. 5 consisted fundamentally in the Allende government's rupture of the constitutional and legal order of the Republic. In fact, that order has not been reestablished by the new regime, but, rather, has been suppressed. The political constitution and the laws are not respected and the ruling junta adheres only to the rules which it accepts or announces itself. The intention of promulgating a new constitution has been announced, whose nature is not known, and not a word has been said regarding the participation of the people in its possible ratification.

6. Although the government has issued several declarations in which it has declared its intention of not returning to the past, of seeking effective social justice, or respecting the rights of the workers and of advancing their participation in the management of the factories in which they work, the markedly right-wing tendencies of the majority of the persons into whose hands has fallen the administration of the nationalized, requisitioned, or taken-over enterprises, as well as the entirety of the agricultural sector, lead us to hear that in fact these declarations have been contradicted.

7. All the foregoing leads to serious doubts regarding the immediate future. For how long will the nation remain deprived of its public liberties? What will be the fate of the workers, farmers, students, intellectuals, and journalists? What socio-economic orientation will prevail?

While the honesty, patriotism, and good faith of the members of the junta and, in general, of the armed forces and the carabineros inspire the confidence that their action will be oriented exclusively to the performance of the announced goals of reestablishing order, beginning reconstruction, and returning to institutional normality, eventually returning power to the people so that it may democratically decide its destiny, it is apparent that they are surrounded by sectors of the economic and political right, partly concealed by the clothing of "gremialismo," as well as by groups of known totalitarian mentality, which has resulted in orienting governmental action toward regressive socio-economic models of a capitalist nature and toward the permanent consolidation of a system of dictatorial government.

IV. Position of the Christian Democratic Party

1. Cognizant of the fact that the total crisis of Chile has placed the nation in a situation of emergency which also requires emergency solutions, the Christian Democratic Party has observed an attitude of understanding toward the new government.

This attitude has expressed itself primarily by the following facts:

a. the Declaration put forth by the Party's leadership on the 12th of September and the public statement made by the National President of the Party three days later, identifying the responsibility of the preceding government for the events which occurred and expressing its confidence in the patriotic statements made by the armed forces;

b. the authorization which we have given to our supporters to contribute to the new government their technical, professional, or functional cooperation, along the lines of our political philosophy, to the tasks of reconstruction, and overcoming the crisis by reestablishing institutions, moral cleansing, and searching for peace and unity among Chileans which are indispensable for the good of the country in this emergency, and;

c. abstaining from expressing publicly, by means which have been in our reach, our profound disagreement with certain of the measures adopted by the junta, especially those referred to in parts 3, 4, and 5 of paragraph III of this document, a restraint we have scrupulously maintained in order not to contribute any further to the deterioration of the external image of Chile.

2. The Party supports the purposes of national reconciliation expressed by the junta, the necessity of basing reconstruction and national progress on the work of all Chileans and the importance that the principle of authority be reestablished. But at the same time it believes it is necessary to point out, in view of the facts which are occurring, that if the noble and patriotic intentions announced by the ruling junta are to be realized, and if the whole national community is to be effectively inspired by them, its actions, and those of its collaborators, must be without hatred or persecutions of persons of differing ideological tendencies, in a spirit of honesty and justice and on a basis of equal allegiance of all concerned to the Constitution and the laws.

No national reconciliation is possible if a part of the national community is excluded and persecuted solely for the ideas that they profess.
There is no real possibility of mobilizing the work of all Chileans in a great creative effort except on the basis of real social justice and participation of all, without abuses or discrimination. There is no effective authority which is not based at one and the same time on moral authority and on the observance of an objective norm, impersonal and general for all, without exceptions.

3. In accordance with the position it has always held, to place the common good of Chile above any sort of interest and any party consideration, the Christian Democratic Party shares in the purposes of healthy nationalism and a rejection of petty politicking that has

been expressed by the junta. However, it also rejects as a grave error and a typically totalitarian deviation the intention of certain people of banning all political activity as contrary to the national interest.

In this hour, in which a few brazen men of known anti-democratic and reactionary tendency attempt to capitalize on the action of the armed forces and the carabineros, we believe it is necessary to remind them and the Chilean public as well as the whole world that it was the democratic political parties, with our parliamentarians, óur grass-roots leaders, our journalists and our militants, who for three long years participated in a hard struggle without quarter to awaken the national conscience to the communist totalitarian menace, to keep alive the critical spirit of the Chileans and strengthen its resistance.

The Christian Democratic Party affirms its right to exist and will defend it. It interprets the patriotic and democratic, humanistic, Christian and communitary ideals of justice and liberty, which are shared by the majority of Chileans. No governmental decision will be able to suppress those ideals nor prevent their expression in one form or another.

The political parties are not killed or paralyzed by decree. So long as the ideas which they express remain in existence, no person and no thing can prevent them from flourishing and guiding in one form or another the life of the people.

4. We are especially concerned that the emergency regime which is imposed by the present situation will not lead to an irreparable lesion in our historical tradition as a free people, a deserved reputation which distinguishes Chile in the society of nations.

In accordance with this criterion, we place special emphasis on the necessity that:

a. the rights of the person be respected, rights which are universally recognized in international agreements to which Chile is signatory and which the political Constitution guarantees to all the inhabitants of our nation. Excesses of rigor, precipitate decisions, stupidity of authorities or secondary functionaries, can constitute intolerable assaults on these rights;

b. the rights of workers and farmers must be respected, as promised, and the existence and character of its union organizations, as well as the Neighborhood Associations, cooperatives, Maternal Centers, student federations and other community organizations;

c. the progress made under previous governments with regard to the nationalization of our basic resources must be retained and consolidated, as well as the extinction of the large landed estates and the abolition of monopolies;

d. we must not move backwards in the process of socialization of the national economy, unless it is done following the norms of justice, efficiency, and real and democratic participation of the workers in the enterprises in which they work;

e. the agrarian reform must be consolidated, turning over expropriated land to the farmers in accordance with the law, promoting the formation and development of agrarian reform cooperatives and furnishing them with all the technical and financial assistance they require to advance agricultural production;

f. the scientific, academic, and cultural autonomy of the universities must be respected; they must be provided with the means they require for their financing so that the academic, student, and university workers' associations may be able to carry on their activities, and;

g. the traditional freedom of cultural expression of our nation must be maintained, in its various literary, artistic, journalistic, and other manifestations.

5. Emergency solutions, by their exceptional nature, cannot be anything but temporary. In no case are they justified once the emergency which gave rise to them has passed.

On more than one occasion, the armed forces and Carabineros have attested that they have assumed power "only for as long as circumstances require" and that, once normality has been reestablished, they will return it to the people to whom it belongs so that they may democratically elect their future rulers.

There will be no lack of those who will seek excuses to prolong indefinitely "the emergency conditions" in order to justify the permanent institutionalization of a dictatorial government.
For our part, we have faith in the honor of our armed forces and Carabinier forces and, cognizant of their patriotism and disinterestedness, are confident that they will not attempt to prolong an emergency regime any longer than is strictly necessary. Which action would constitute an historical error having the worst consequences, because it could precipitate Chile precisely into the danger which their intervention was intended to prevent.

6. In response to the announcement of the possibility of a new political Constitution, we affirm the principle that the Constitutional power belongs uniquely to the people and can be exercized only by those whom it assigns to represent it. Nobody can arrogate to himself the right to impose a constitution on Chile. The nation's history, moreover, reveals clearly enough that improvised constitutions which have attempted to impose theoretical models which have not developed out of social reality itself, and have not been accepted democratically by the people, have not managed to survive.

We admit the usefulness of modernizing our political regime; we believe it is useful to turn to the most capable men in the nation, of all social and economic sectors and without regard to party affiliation, to study the matter and to make proposals; however, we reject any attempt to impose hastily any formula which has not been previously discussed in a democratic manner and approved by the people.

7. These criteria, which are the expression of the principles of our doctrine and of our patriotic feelings, will inspire our attitude and that of our militants in the face of the circumstances existing in Chile and to the direction of the authorities who have assumed the government.

While adhering to our principles, the Party will not refuse the government any patriotic cooperation. Neither will we refuse to acknowledge our obligation to struggle as Chileans against all that which we honestly and in conscience believe to be prejudicial to its people.

Faithful to our democratic and revolutionary vocation, we shall continue to struggle—regardless of the circumstances—to build in our nation a society of workers which shall be personalist and communitarian, truly just and free, inspired by the principles of Christian humanism.

Renewing our faith in Chile and in its people, our faith in the patriotism and honesty of our armed forces and Carabineros, our loyalty to the principles we have always had, we call upon each of our militants, on the basis expressed above and proceeding according to their conscience, to do their duty as Chileans and as Christian Democrats.

To the People of Chile

The following is a clandestine statement made by the directorate of the Communist Party of Chile on October 11, 1973. It was smuggled out of Santiago by means of a secret routing.

The military coup of September 11 plunged the country into a state of terror and savagery such as history has never known before. The brutality and vindictiveness with which all democratic movements, especially the working-class movement, are being suppressed have no precedent either in our country or elsewhere in Latin America. The present bloodbath is comparable only to that which followed the coup in Indonesia.

The military junta's every act is a complete negation of what the forces in opposition to the people's government professed to support. They talked about democracy, yet are imposing a dictatorship on the nation. They talked about freedom, yet are setting up concentration camps. They talked about respect for the individual, yet people are being summarily shot daily. They said they stood for pluralism and autonomy of the universities, yet they have placed them under the control of the military.

The real situation is this:

A fascist dictatorship with all its attributes of criminal actions and abuses has been established in the country.

The fascist junta represents no national or patriotic movement. It is anti-patriotic in essence and acts against the interests of Chile as an independent state. The junta is a fascist instrument of imperialism and the internal reaction.

A few hours after the coup the military junta declared martial law, trampling on the Constitution and the National Congress.

Immediately after this the proceedings of the National Congress were suspended until "further notice." This was soon followed by an edict dissolving both chambers of Congress and declaring the credentials of the senators and deputies invalid. Those who only yesterday had gone out of their way vociferously to proclaim at every opportunity their support of the legislative authority now were silent. We are referring to the President of the Senate, Senor Frei, and the Speaker of the Chamber of Deputies, Senor Pareto, who obediently submitted to this lawlessness.

On September 24 the junta announced the dissolution of the municipal councils, which, like Parliament, had been chosen by free election. Today these bodies of local government are appointed by the military junta.

After this the junta decided to appoint only military men as rectors of universities, to remove from them all Marxist instructors and to ban the teaching of Marxism. An end was put to university autonomy. Manhunts are staged and people hounded in an openly fascist manner.

All civil liberties have been abolished. Freedom of assembly and association and freedom of speech and of the press have been completely done away with.

Punitive operations reached an incredibly brutal pitch. The civilian population, especially people living in people's settlements and outlying districts of towns, are the victims of repressions of all kinds, which have evoked general indignation. The immunity of the home is violated. Massacres are staged. Books are being burned as was done in Germany at the height of Hitlerism. The number of the summarily shot runs into the hundreds.

Martial law has been supplemented with a decree under which death sentences are being handed down.

In view of all these facts, which testify to the establishment of a fascist-type dictatorship, one must ask: what do the Christian Democrats say about all this? What has happened to their former opposition to any variety of anti-democratic development? What has happened to their favorable attitude towards ideological and political pluralism?

We know that a group of Christian Democratic Party leaders and parliamentarians headed by men like Radomiro Tomic, Bernardo Leighton, Renan Fuentealba and others have taken a dissenting stand. They have remained true to their principles and have publicly condemned the military coup and its consequences. This is to their credit and we believe that they express the views of the absolute majority of Christian Democrat rank and file so outrageously betrayed by their official leaders, who were involved in the conspiracy.

All that the junta has done was planned in cold blood in advance. The putschists began with the bombing and destruction of the La Moneda palace—an act of barbarism for which they will never be forgiven. The totally unjustified bombing of President Allende's residence, the military operations conducted at factories and workers' settlements, the decrees of the junta and the arrest of emerge from the trials and battles ahead stronger than ever.

But the people will once again return to power, and when they do, they will, of course, be under no obligation to restore all the institutions that existed previously. The people will adopt a new constitution, draw up new codes and laws, issue new decrees, establish new state bodies and institutions, build a legally-constituted state of a higher type than that which was strangled by the military coup. It will be a legally-constituted state in which freedom of conscience and opinion will be respected, all norms of humanity observed, but in which there will be no place for laws providing cover for fascism, economic sabotage or subversive actions.

After what has happened the people of Chile are entitled to make it their aim to create armed forces and a police of a new type, or at least cleanse the army, the police and the judiciary of fascist elements and thereby rule out any repetition of the tragedy that has befallen our people today.

The ordeals that are now the lot of the Chileans will not be in vain. Some of the institutions in which many sincerely believed have today proved themselves to be rotten to the core. Who would think of supporting the existing judicial system or a parliament that condemned itself by becoming a party to the anti-government conspiracy?

There are also other questions that have to be reconsidered by the revolutionary and democratic forces in order to work out a common position.

Of course, the nearly three years of Popular Unity government must also be subjected to a critical and self-critical analysis. Important reforms were effected in this time, but serious mistakes too were committed. Grave damage was caused by the activities of the leftist elements and reformist tendencies, which at times made themselves felt in the work of the Popular Unity government. The Communist Party is absolutely convinced that its policy of unconditional support of the Popular Unity government, its work to achieve mutual understanding with other democratic forces, especially at grassroots level, its striving to inspire confidence in the middle strata of the population, its efforts to direct the main blow against the principal enemies—imperialism and internal reaction—its persistent labors to strengthen the alliance of the Communists and the Socialists, the unity of the working class and understanding among the Popular Unity parties, its efforts to increase production and raise the productivity of labor, to heighten the profitability of enterprises of the state sector, and to ensure strict observance of labor discipline were all components of a correct general policy.

On the other hand, the Communist Party feels that this is not the time to engage in debates about the mistakes committed by the government and the Popular Unity bloc thousands of citizens—this was all carefully thought out beforehand. As the newspaper *El Mercurio* has admitted, the junta employed the fascist blitzkrieg tactic, the tactic of a lightning blow delivered simultaneously everywhere in order, apart from everything else, to sow panic among the civilian population.

The whole world knows that our country's economic and financial difficulties were due not only to the government's mistakes, although these too played their part, but also to the fact that it inherited from previous governments a huge external debt, a backward agriculture, a weak infrastructure, and also to the decline of copper prices in the course of two years, the devaluation of the dollar, the ending of U.S. credits, economic sabotage, the enormous losses caused by transport strikes, and the adoption of budget laws and increase of wages without adequate financial measures to back them up.

Imperialism and the oligarchy did not forgive President Allende and the Popular Unity bloc for nationalizing the extractive industries, carrying forward the agrarian reform, nationalizing the banks, and creating a state sector of the economy.

In a vain attempt to vindicate themselves before Chilean and world public opinion, they concocted the fantastic lie that the armed forces were faced with the alternative of either taking action or allowing themselves to be attacked and, above all, beheaded by militarized detachments the Popular Unity bloc had allegedly set up.

According to this fabrication, the Popular Unity bloc allegedly was preparing to carry out this scheme on Monday, September 17. Imperialism and its fascist servitors within the country resorted to this crude concoction to counteract the feeling of outrage their foul crimes have evoked throughout the world. The lie was so incredible that the head of the military junta, General

Pinochet, said, as was reported by the press on September 18: "It is quite possible that they really were preparing a coup. There were so many rumors, so many people who sought to spread doubt and alarm among the population."

The new rulers fear the people. And so they institute a state of emergency and a curfew, unleash a reign of terror, bring television and radio broadcasting under their complete control, ban the left press, abolish the rights of the trade unions, persecute dissenters and outlaw the Marxist parties. All this with the approval and the participation of many pseudodemocrats.

As always, we shall place the emphasis on the organization, the unity and the struggle of the masses, on the growth of their political consciousness. The confusion and despondency which may now be observed among certain sections of the people are obviously of a transient nature. The working class and the entire people will as a whole and each of its political parties in particular. There is a time for everything. To concentrate now on such a discussion would jeopardize the unity of the people's parties at a time when unity is the main condition of success in their struggle against the military dictatorship, and in jointly resolving the new tasks facing the working class and the people.

The military junta has outlawed Marxism, our Party and all other parties that are guided in their activities by the teachings of Marx, Engels and Lenin. More, it is seeking to make it appear as if the interests of the Chilean nation are alien to us.

Our Party has been in existence for 53 years. It traces its origins to the period preceding the first world war when, in 1912, the great Chilean revolutionary and patriot Luis Recabarren founded the Socialist Workers' Party.

Those who know something about the development of Chilean society know that each class in the country has had one or more political parties representing its aspirations and interests.

Many of the members and leaders of our Party have become the victims of persecution by the military junta. But despite this the Communist Party and the splendid Young Communist League of Chile will courageously carry forward their battle standards. Our Party will be steeled still more in the difficult conditions ahead. It will emerge stronger and more prestigious than ever from the struggle.

We have suffered heavy losses but we shall regain our strength.

In these difficult days Pablo Neruda died. His death was unquestionably hastened by the crimes now being committed in Chile. Pablo Neruda was not only one of the greatest poets of our time, he was a true Communist, a member of the Central Committee of our Party. He wrote inspired poems about the exploits of the Araucanian heroes, the heroes of the struggle for independence, and the heroes of the working-class struggle—Recabarren and Lafferte; he sang of our fields, the sea and our endless rocky coastline. A man of great culture, keen mind and broad vision, he dedicated his poetry to the great cause of peace and socialism the world over. His heart was open to people of all latitudes, all races and all languages. But deepest of all was his love for his own people and country, for his native land, for the austere nature of Northern Chile, the rain-swept Andes, for Valparaiso, for its people and its hills.

A few days after the death of Pablo Neruda, Luis Corvalan, the General Secretary of our Party, was arrested by the usurpers of power.

Luis Corvalan's life must be saved. The people must secure his immediate release.

Despite the strict censorship introduced by the military junta, our people have learned of the protest voiced throughout the world against the fascist military coup.

In the ranks of the fighters for unity there is a place for

every man and woman, young and old, in our country, even those who yesterday, under the influence of reactionary propaganda, were in the opposition.

The struggle will end in the final victory of Chile. Our people will once again resume their creative constructive labors, the young people will return to the university auditoriums to debate and to learn, and peace and tranquility will be restored to Chilean homes.

The MIR Analyzes the Coup

This interview with Miguel Enriquez, the Secretary-General of the Movement of the Revolutionary Left (MIR), took place at an undisclosed place shortly after the military coup of September 11, 1973.

Question: In your opinion why was Allende's government overthrown?

Enriquez: The crisis of the system of class domination had been developing for years in Chile, and crystallized with the election of the Popular Unity government. Allende's government sharpened the crisis of the state political institutions and the internal crisis of the bourgeoisie, and at the same time increased the strength of the mass movement. All this generated conditions which made possible the conquest of power by the workers and the proletarian revolution, if the government had been used as an instrument of the struggles of the workers. But the reformist strategy attempted by the

Popular Unity government was imprisoned within the rules of the game of the bourgeoisie, and did not try to injure all of the dominating classes. Instead it sought an alliance with one sector of the bourgeoisie. It did not seek support in the revolutionary workers' organizations which had created their own institutions. It rejected an alliance with soldiers and non-commissioned officers, and instead sought to fortify itself within the capitalist state. The Popular Unity government looked for an allliance with the officers of the armed forces, and with a fraction of the bourgeoisie. The reformist illusion permitted the dominating classes to fortify themselves in the superstructure of the state and from there incite a reactionary offensive. That offensive at first was based on the bosses' organizations, then on the petit bourgeoisie, and finally on the officers of the armed forces, leading to the bloody coup d'etat and the repression of the workers. The price of the reformist illusion was paid and is being paid today by the workers, their leaders and their parties, who tragically and heroically defended that illusion up to the last minute. The phrase of the French revolutionary of the 18th century, Saint Just, "He who carries out a revolution only half way is only digging his own tomb," is dramatically confirmed today.

Question: In your opinion does the defeat of the left mean the end of the struggle for socialism in Chile for a long time to come?

Enriquez: We don't feel that now is the moment to revive old differences within the left, but at the same time we feel that it is necessary that the workers and the left learn all the lessons that the Chilean experience offers, so as to never again make the same mistakes. Therefore I want to be explicit: in Chile neither the left, nor socialism, nor the revolution have been defeated. In Chile a reformist illusion has come to its tragic end, the illusion of modifying socio-economic structures and carrying out a revolution with the consent and passivity of those whose interests were most injured, the dominating classes.

In any case, the struggle, far from being over, is just beginning. It will be long and hard. The mass movement and the left have not been crushed. Under the new conditions the force of the workers and the left in general, at first weakened, then recuperating, tends once again to gain strength, as sectors of the petit bourgeoisie join the struggle against dictatorship. The petit bourgeoisie, which yesterday was against the Popular Unity government, is today reacting against the bloody fascist repression of the junta, and against the regressive and unpopular measures imposed by the military. There is already a solid and vast popular resistance to the fascist dictatorship, and it will progressively develop every day.

Question: The military junta says that it intervened only after two branches of the state (the judicial and legislative) had declared the illegitimacy of Allende's government, and in order to prevent a Plan Z with which the left proposed to exterminate all democratic sectors, the armed forces officers, and even Allende. What is your opinion of this?

Enriquez: After having bombed the Moneda (the presidential palace), the junta takes pains to point out that this is not a military coup d'etat, but instead a "military pronouncement," and then adds that the armed forces are "professional and not deliberative institutions." They claim that they intervened because such intervention was asked for by a fundamental part of the state, the Parliament, and then proceed to immediately close it down. They claim that their objective is to "restore legality," at the same time they are creating dozens of concentration camps throughout the country where they jail dozens of thousands of Chileans for being "Marxists." They claim that the military movement was in order to end the sectarianism which was suffocating Chile, and immediately they outlaw and pursue the 44 per cent of the population which was leftist. They claim that their objective is to reconstruct the economy of the country, which they do by machine-gunning factories and firing thousands of workers for being "Marxists." They claim that they have "intervened" in order to prevent a "Plan Z" that would have meant the death of Allende on September 19, and they kill him ahead of time on September 11. They claim that their military action was in order to defend human rights, and they have executed at least a thousand people and caused the deaths of tens of thousands. They claim that the fundamental goal of their action is to defend "national values" and in pursuit of that goal they make bonfires in the streets to burn books and sack the house of Pablo Neruda. They intervene militarily in the universities, and troops search the house of the Cardinal.

All this, according to them, is in defense of the workers and their conquests, but the first thing they do is dissolve workers' organizations, then they fire thousands of workers, cut off over-time pay, increase the hours in the work day, and create a system of what is really forced labor. They have frozen salaries, increased prices, and at least in the province of Linares they are returning farms to their former owners. They are naming former owners as government managers in the factories of the state sector. They claim to look for the weapons of the "extremists" which are a danger for the security of the "citizens," and then they carry out genocide against workers' neighborhoods, reformed farms, the factories, and the universities.

Chile is today a country submitted by its armed forces to a regime similar to that of a country occupied by foreign forces. The country is under a "state of seige." Its cities are under curfew; there are military courts without appeals, working under a "Wartime Military Code of Justice." There exists massive imprisonment of the population, violent searches, generalized torture, summary executions, virtual pogroms against foreigners, etc. The officers of the armed forces of Chile have declared war against the people of Chile. We have in the decade of the '70s a version even more grotesque and backwards of Hitler's fascism.

The difference between these fascist gorillas and their Hitlerian predecessors, if there is a difference, is that the former do not have the courage to take responsibility for their crimes, but try to cover them up behind lies and publicity campaigns like the Plan Z, and behind a histrionic pretense of legality.

Question: In your opinion what is the future of this government?

Enriquez: It won't last. Chile does not have a powerful and expansionist bourgeoisie like Germany's of past decades, nor does it have the economic potential of a Brazil. World and Latin American conditions of this decade are not the same as those of the past decade: today the socialist camp is stronger; the Indochinese people have inflicted important defeats on imperialism in Vietnam, Laos, and Cambodia; the internal crisis of the bourgeoisie in North America and Latin America is continually greater; the mass movement is growing stronger in Latin America and is still strong in Chile. The Chilean fascist dictatorship will continue to stain its hands with blood, will adopt measures which will be even more repressive and unpopular, will suffer even greater internal contradictions, and will come into conflict with some sectors of the bourgeoisie. At the same time the popular resistance to the dictatorship will grow amongst the workers, and finally overthrow the junta. Then, after the working class and the people have gone through the most dramatic and the best political education possible—that of the iron grip of the bourgeoisie and imperialist dictatorship—democratic liberties will be restored and the path will open towards a true revolutionary process led by workers and peasants.

Question: In your opinion and according to your information did the U.S.A. participate in the coup, as has been claimed?

Enriquez: One month before the coup d'etat we denounced on a national network of radios the participation of a member of the U.S. Embassy in a meeting on a cruiser of the navy in the port of Arica on May 20 this year. This meeting occurred at 1 A.M., with the high command of the navy and various officers of high rank in the northern army division. We also denounced that in the months of June and July an officer of the U.S. Naval Intelligence accompanied every ship of the fleet. None of this was even denied by the navy.

Each step of the reactionary plot was directed and planned by the Brazilian Military Mission and the U.S. Naval Intelligence.

Question: What do you consider are the tasks for this period?

Enriquez: In general: unite all the left and all democratic sectors which are ready to struggle against the dictatorship; reorganize the mass movement in new ways, and develop popular resistance to the dictatorship in all its forms throughout the country.

Those who declared war were the fascist high-level officers of the armed forces, and not us. They have determined the rules of the game. They have gone to the extreme of establishing a norm which is extremely bloody and which has not been established in any other type of war. All who resist are executed, which in other words means a war to the death, a war without prisoners.

It will be a long and difficult struggle but it is certain that the working class and the people, with their vanguards leading them, will triumph. Many have already fallen in battle and many more will fall, but they will be and have been replaced; the struggle will not end until the fascist junta is overthrown, democratic liberties have been restored, and a path is opened towards a revolutionary process led by workers and peasants.

Question: What is your impression of the international solidarity received by the Chilean left and what tasks would you suggest for those who are outside Chile and want to help?

Enriquez: The international solidarity has been fundamental. The fact that numerous governments have rejected the coup d'etat and the fact that democratic and revolutionary sectors around the world have mobilized against Chilean fascists has been an enormous help. Especially important has been the solidarity of the socialist camp, of the Cuban revolution, of democratic and revolutionary sectors in Europe and in Latin America, and that of the People's Revolutionary Army in Argentina, the National Liberation Movement (Tupamaros) in Uruguay, and the Army of National Liberation in Bolivia. The international pressure sharpens the internal contradictions of the fascist junta, and the contradictions between it and other sectors, at the same time that this pressure occasionally is able to neutralize at least some of the most bloody and brutal maneuvers of the dictatorship.

As far as what can be done from the outside for the anti-gorilla and anti-fascist struggle, everything is useful: publicizing as much as possible the crimes and the bestialities of the regime; gaining political and material support for the resistance; organizing protest rallies; and multiplying the solidarity campaigns. In as much as it is possible other governments must be stopped from recognizing Chilean fascism and sabotage outside of Chile must be encouraged. For example, refusing to unload cargo from Chilean ships, etc. One of the principal tasks today is to demand the immediate freedom of the General Secretary of the Chilean Communist Party, Luis Corvalan, who is at this moment in jail, and to demand the end of the executions and the tortures of prisoners.

Question: Do you want to add anything else?

Enriquez: Yes, today, the day of the heroic guerilla (October 8, the day of the death of Che Guevara) we want to render homage to Salvador Allende who gave his life defending his convictions, and to the thousands of heros and martyrs in the plazas, streets, factories, neighborhoods, and countryside, coming from all leftist organizations, and to those workers who spilled their blood in combating fascism.

We want to render homage to those who are still being killed and tortured. We render a special homage to the member of the Central Committee and founder of the Movement of the Revolutionary Left [MIR], head of the Regional Committee of Valdivia, 24 years old, Fernando Krausse, and to our militant and head of the Local Committee in Panguipulli, Jose Gregorio Liendo, both shot several days ago by the fascist gorillas in the province of Valdivia, an area in which the armed resistance in the countryside continues.

A Conservative's Prescription for Chile's Future

Below appear some of the thoughts of one of the leaders of the Conservative National Party, Senator Francisco Bulnes. It appeared in the November 2, 1973 issue of the conservative daily, La Segunda.

Question: What type of political system do you believe Chile should have in the future?

Bulnes: I am a democrat and partisan to the belief that things should be done within a juridical framework, under the protection of the law, and not subject to arbitrary things. I do not see the present system of government as a definite solution, which is destined to prevail for much longer. What is taking place today are painful corrective measures, which have to be applied in order that liberty and democracy may again sprout in Chile.

Question: Within what frame do you visualize that new juridical order for the future?

Bulnes: The first and fundamental thing is to apply to the system measures which are corrective and efficient, because the system was in a decline and a crisis. Well now, I do not believe that correcting the system, establishing a pure democracy, necessarily entails rewriting a whole, new constitution. The necessary changes perhaps do not require very many words, but they may definitely cause a profound effect.

Some feel that the primary act should be to substitute the regime of political parties—of a Congress with different current ideologies—with a corporate system. I do not agree with them.

In the first place, no one would be able to determine, in a Congress of such a composition, how the different representatives of the guilds [Gremias] would participate: how would the professors be in relation to the dentists, to the metallurgists or the street vendors?

Before anything, it must be clarified that I am perfectly aware of the part that the guilds have played in the previous government, of their decisiveness and combative spirit. But let us return to normal times. The guilds are substantially representatives of economic interests, or, at least, of a very determined sector of the society. A Corporate Chamber would not integrate the country but would instead devote itself to the competition of the different interests of these sectors.

We must keep in mind that all the vices that may penetrate a political party can also occur in a guild. And perhaps with greater ease.

Question: How then, should the new constitutional regime be?

Bulnes: With the political parties as a base. Of course, it will be necessary to take adequate steps to prevent these parties from being liable to corruption and from being, essentially, partisan and political busybodies. One of the fundamental ways of achieving this would be to depoliticize the Senate as much as possible. This Chamber would have to be split from the direct electoral interest and the compromises which are derived thereof.

It would be necessary to establish that the Senators must be elected by all the Republic and only by electoral college vote, in this manner separating them from the assembly. The Senators should not be re-elected until a complete term has transpired, nor should they be elected as President of the Republic while they are Senators, and until a certain number of years had passed since they ceased their membership.

This would impede political leaders with presidential ambitions or those who have a full political career ahead of them to be in the Senate. This way, the Senate would be composed of a select body of people who would not pursue electoral interests, who would be devoid of partisanship, and who would wish to complete a political career.

Question: What would be the function of such a Senate?

Bulnes: They would function as the previous one had, but, in addition, they would be able to call a plebiscite with respect to the President. For this, they would need a majority vote since, in any case, practice has demonstrated that nothing is accomplished with a two-thirds vote.

The Senate may, once during its mandate, submit to the plebiscite a record of the actions of the President. This way, we would prevent events from occurring the way they did with Salvador Allende—a Caesar who trampled the other powers of the state, and against whom there was no legal recourse.

Another indispensable reform would be the establishment, in all types of popular elections, of a second round. In the first round, only the one with an absolute majority would be elected.

The principle on which I base this is reasonable: a government or legislator should be elected by an absolute majority. This system permits the democratic forces to run independently of each other the first time around, and the second time, unites their forces against Marxist elements. And this is very logical. The differences between democrats would always be minor compared to the ones between democrats and Marxists.

We must also reform what has been, hitherto, the cancer

of our legislation: legislative instability, especially concerning economic matters. This instability kills confidence and makes it impossible to have intensive development.

Modern experience shows that the more developed countries are the ones with more stability in their economic legislation. We would have to establish a group of norms in the Constitution, and vigorously restrain parliamentary initiative in this aspect. Just as in England where this parliamentary initiative practically does not exist.

Question: What would be the situation of the Marxists; should they continue functioning outside the law?

Bulnes: I believe that it is impossible to prohibit the participation of people who, in one manner or another, are Marxist. But, of course, some should be exiled· those who manifest Marxist or Leninist methods, those who oppose the established system and consider any means to attain power as legitimate. Democracy should be able to defend itself against such people.

The Marxists are skillful, they disguise themselves, they are imitative, they protect themselves under the shelter of other groups. Is this not beginning the cycle again?

It is possible that with a return to democratic life, this would give impetus to the cycle. It depends on the corrective factors. But the non-democratic systems get corrupted and reach worse degradation. Sometimes there rises to the top a providential man, as was the case of Franco in Spain, but this is not what happens for each nation. In general, the non-democratic regimes succumb after a short while, under the weight of their errors and corruption.

This is not to say that the present regime (the military junta) will continue for only a short period of time. I understand the grave illness of Chile. We must de-toxify Chile from the venom that was spread by Marxism and cure her damaged economy. All this takes years and would not have occurred in a democratic regime. How many years? I don't know. Hopefully, the shortest time possible.

Question: But you were one of those who were convinced that there would be no way out politically?

Bulnes: Absolutely convinced. I only began believing in this type of solution after the parliamentary elections (March, 1973). I believed that with the two-thirds vote in the Senate, the opposition would destroy Salvador Allende. Those two-thirds alone would have forced Allende to alter his actions fundamentally. We didn't receive the two-thirds vote.

Believe me when I say that I am not advocating that a constitution be brought out right now. It has to be the result of this new process through which we are living.

Question: Do you believe that public opinion is now dormant and that they do not want to know anything more about politics for a long while?

Bulnes: It is very difficult to still public opinion. It has only been subdued in order to give the military junta the opportunity to govern, and it is in a state of suspension, keeping silent and not criticizing. But it is watchful.

CULTURE AND RELIGION UNDER THE JUNTA

No sector of Chilean national life has been more visited by turmoil than the universities and private secondary schools. The military has assumed control of the St. George School, run by the Holy Cross order of Indiana, which is one of Santiago's largest private secondary schools. As the Kandell article illustrates, this disruption has had an even deeper effect on Chile's once prestigious university system. In the article titled "Portrait of a Book Burner," the scene switches to Valparaiso, the home of the Chilean navy and the setting for much of the military plotting against the Allende government. Here we see the junta's educational policy being implemented at the famed Santa Maria Technical University. Following this we have a personal account by a British citizen, who was on the faculty of Austral University, concerning the manner in which faculty members were purged from the institution after the military overthrow. Turning to Chile's religious institutions and their fate under the new government, we begin an investigation of Chile's Jewish community by presenting an article by Rabbi Rosenthal who is an expert on Latin American affairs for B'nai B'rith. This article was written during the early days of the Allende administration. Next we come upon a disturbing signed contribution which appeared on the editorial page of **La Prensa,** *the official newspaper of the Christian Democratic Party, several weeks before the coup. Following is an article that first appeared in the German magazine* **Der Stern.** *It concerns itself with the prison island of Quiriquina and some of the events that took place there several weeks after the coup. It should be noted that the leadership of the Chilean Jewish community has maintained that the junta has not sanctioned anti-semitic acts and that its attitude has been respectful and correct. Turning to the status of the Catholic church, we have an account of Cardinal Raul Silva Henriquez' relationship with the new military junta. It should be remembered that in spite of the apparent accommodations that he is making to it, for most of the Allende period he displayed a cordiality to the coalition government. The next report relates some of the clerical casualties that have resulted from the coup and also refers to those who were forced to seek asylum or leave the country. Our final presentation in this section is another reference to Chile's Cardinal. Here he affirmatively comments upon the possibility of coexistence between Catholicism and Marxism.*

The Plight of the Intellectuals

JONATHAN KANDELL

This article appeared in the New York Times *of November 14, 1973 under the title, "A Wide Anti-Marxist Purge in Chile is Shaking the Universities."*

Two months after the military coup that overthrew President Salvador Allende Gossens, a vast anti-Marxist purge is shaking the Chilean university system to its foundations.

Military rectors have been appointed to head most institutions in the system, which has a total enrollment of 128,000. Leftist professors and students by the thousands have been swept off campuses, and many may face permanent expulsion.

Some universities and graduate departments, particularly in the social sciences, have been closed while the authorities sift out supposed left-wing extremists and Marxist courses.

Even though classes have resumed under a surface calm in most institutions, the pent up hatred of the last three years of political rivalries has exploded in an ugly campaign of denunciations, mixing personal abuse with ideological discrimination.

In the University of Concepcion, the most important academic center south of Santiago, about 6,000 of 16,000 students and hundreds of professors have been suspended.

The eastern campus of the University of Chile in Santiago, the country's largest and most impressive university, has been closed because of reported Marxist penetration of its social science and political science departments. About 8,000 students there—most of them leftists—have had their careers cut short, at least temporarily.

In the prestigious University of Chile Law School, 44 of 360 professors and about 70 students have been suspended.

Some 1,500 students in the university's schools of fine arts, music and architecture have been suspended, as well as about 100 professors.

Military Tells Why

Since the Sept. 11 coup, in which President Allende died, the junta has dissolved the national Congress, banned Marxist parties and declared other political parties in "indefinite recess."

"After an analysis of the grave and conflicting problems of the universities, which have practically impeded the normal development of academic activities, the military junta has decided to decree the reorganization of universities throughout the country," a recent government communique declared in bringing to an end a long tradition of university autonomy.

The universities have traditionally been springboards to political power. Student leaders often doubled as youth leaders of political parties.

The University of Concepcion's social science department, for example, gave birth to the extremist Revolutionary Movement of the Left, which led the illegal seizures of farms and factories in recent years. The University of Chile's law faculty, on the other hand, was a conservative stronghold that produced many of the crusty stalwarts of the court system and the anti-Marxist legislative majority.

Like every other institution during the last year of the Marxist coalition government, the university system became bitterly polarized between leftists and anti-Marxists.

Although the leftists held a clear edge in political power in many universities when President Allende assumed office in 1970, coalitions of moderate and right-wing students later gained the upper hand.

In the final months of the Marxist government, pitched battles were fought on several campuses between supporters and opponents of President Allende. Often the rival groups took turns occupying university buildings.

"The student movement was a shambles even before Allende fell," said Carlos Latorre, an engineering student in his final year and national leader of university students affiliated with the Christian Democrats, a center-left party that opposed the Allende government.

"This was an insane asylum," said German Vidal, a conservative and a professor of commercial law at the University of Chile. "I crave for order and discipline and authority. I'm sick of counsels and bureaucracy and confrontations. All I want is to have somebody on top who will make decisions, even if they are bad decisions."

Support for Purge

The military officials who are making the decisions on campuses now have been able to tap this widespread law and order sentiment among anti-Marxists to carry out their purge with a semblance of popular support.

While military rectors have closed whole departments or universities that were leftist strongholds, they have also encouraged right-wing professors and students to denounce Marxists.

Almost every department in the University of Chile has been assigned a "prosecutor"—in most cases, a law professor—to receive written or oral denunciations of reported extremists. The accused is not allowed to face his accuser.

"If I don't do this, somebody worse will," said a professor of constitutional law, as he lamely explained his decison to act as a prosecutor in a science department. "The way I see it, it is a choice between throwing out some innocent Marxists and throwing them all out."

While the prosecutor mulled over his blacklist, 10 of the department's professors left the country, joining a growing exodus of left-wing academicians, particularly in the sciences.

"As you can see everything here is virtually normalized," said Angel Bate, an administrator at the State Technical University, where 150 professors have been expelled and 300 of 12,000 students have been suspended.

Soldiers with machine guns patrolled the campus and stood guard outside the office of Col. Eugenio Reyes, the new rector.

Despite the long tradition of libertarianism and political activity among university students here, Colonel Reyes was optimistic that the military could maintain its control over the campuses for several years.

"I think students will come to realize that we are not trying to repress anyone for repression's sake," he explained. "We are trying to apoliticize the universities, just as we are trying to apoliticize the country. All we are asking them to do is to study."

Manchester Guardian (weekly), October 6, 1973: Portrait of a Book Burner

If the new military authorities are worried by the international reception given to the reports of book-burning in Santiago, no trace of this concern has yet breached Valparaiso, Chile's second largest city and the country's major port.

Valparaiso is the home of the Chilean navy, traditionally the most reactionary of the three branches of the Chilean armed forces. Its representative on the ruling junta, Admiral Jose Toribio Merino, has already distinguished himself by his attempts to ban miniskirts and women's trousers—successfully vetoed by the other members of the junta.

Now, in Valparaiso, where the navy has absolute control, it is giving the country an object lesson in how to stage a right-wing coup. The principal task is to root out anything connected with Marxism.

Of the universities, Admiral Arturo Troncoso explained to me: "We are going to clean up all the Marxism inside." The admiral is the navy's director-general of personnel, but with training at Newport, Rhode Island, and a spell in the Chilean Embassy in Washington, he is clearly destined for higher things.

"Marxism has been outlawed, so of course we have been burning Marxist books," the admiral said to me.

"Marxism is obsolete as we can see from its results here. It is not capable of producing the well-being of the state."

I pointed out that it was the Marxist parties rather than Marxism itself that had been outlawed, and in any case many books had been burned that had nothing to do with Marxism. "That must have been a mistake," said the admiral with a laugh. "Everyone makes mistakes."

In the Santa Maria Technical University I found much the same story. The university, like the other two in Valparaiso, has been closed and soldiers guard the gates of its ivy-covered "Jacobean" frontage. A retired but youthful naval commander, Captain Juan Naylor, has been put in to reorganize it.

On the mantelpiece of the rector's room which he had taken over, was a medallion inscribed with the words of the university's founder—a rich Chilean called Federico Santa Maria who made his fortune speculating in sugar during the First World War. "It is the task of the privileged classes," said the inscription, "to help the intellectual development of the proletariat."

Captain Naylor apologized for the fact that the library was shut. "The librarians have been working for four days getting rid of all the Marxist literature," he said. "Now they are having a rest." Asked where the library was, he replied: "In truth, I have never been there."

The Santa Maria University was taken over by the navy at four o'clock in the morning of the day of the coup. Captain Naylor believes that it is his task to eliminate politics from the university. "We shall do this first by destroying Marxism, and secondly by destroying every kind of politics."

Captain Naylor said that he had now formed a new university council "without any political tendency. All the Marxists have gone."

Asked how he knew who the Maxists were, he replied: "First, through their previous activity, and secondly through information we receive."

According to Admiral Troncoso there is a black list in Valparaiso of three or four thousand people who are regarded by the new regime as being dangerous.

One load of prisoners has already left Valparaiso on board the Miapu for the reopened concentration camp at Pisagua in the north, last used when the Communist Party was banned in 1947.

Admiral Troncoso said: "Anyone in the public service who was there for political reasons and not a bureaucrat will be sacked. Members of Marxist parties will keep their jobs for the time being, but will be under observation. Mere sympathizers of the Popular Unity can continue working."

Also based in Valparaiso, the intellectual power house of the "Chilean road to fascism," is the newly-appointed Minister of Education, Admiral Hugo Castro. Formerly the director of the naval school, he, too, believes that it is his job to remove politics from the universities.

According to Admiral Castro, the country's educational system needs more equipment and new techniques. "We must encourage industry and technology," he said, "we have too many people studying sociology and philosophy."

These latter faculties are, of course, the ones that were dominated by the left. They will not be reopened.

Faculty Purge at Austral University: An Eyewitness Account

MARIO RINVOLUCRI

The following report on conditions at the Austral University situated in the southern city of Valdivia was written on October 3, 1973 and was passed along by an American educational foundation operating in Latin America. Mr. Rinvolucri holds a B.A. from Oxford University.

According to the quality newspaper *La Opinion* of Buenos Aires, there are 180 professors from the Universidad Tecnica del Estado still held incommunicado in the national stadium in Chile's capital, Santiago. The figures for those killed in the army's brutal pounding of the Universidad Tecnica's central buildings in Santiago on September 11th vary between a low of 200 and a high of 585. It can be said without exaggeration that this, the country's second largest higher educational establishment, was "put out of action" by direct military attack.

The Austral University of Chile in Valdivia has also deserved special attention from the military. Two weeks before the bloody coup, the School of Philosophy and Letters, made up of a leftist majority faculty, was the object of a thorough search for arms. The only thing the soldiers found were a few bottles of naphtha on the side of the river which flows by the campus which had been tossed there by some young members of the Comando Rolando Matus (an extreme right youth movement), who without excessive conviction tried to attack the university campus last June.

On the morning of September 11th, the day of the military coup, a contingent of soldiers ordered all professors, employees, and students to leave the university campus and controlled all accesses to the campus with heavy machine guns. During the week, beginning the 17th of September, professors were permitted to return to their offices, but the soldiers spitefully searched out those professors, who had been individualized as leftists by the wife of the then vice-rector, Mrs. Gladys Santos de Henriquez. The second half of September also brought about numerous denunciations of professors. Dean Guillermo Araya, who founded the School of Philosophy and Letters fourteen years ago under the conservative administration of Jorge Allessandri and who was a candidate for the Presidency of the University last June, was jailed as was his wife, general inspector of the only Girls' High School in Valdivia. Dr. Grinor Rojo, U.S. educated, of the Spanish Department, had the same fate. Professor Carlos Opazo, also of the Spanish Department, was imprisoned and tortured.

One of the things that has characterized the psychological warfare of this coup has been its xenophobia. The foreign heads of university departments underwent arrests and investigations. One of them was Dr. Osvaldo Reig, an Argentine geneticist, and the other, Dr. Peter Weinberger, a West German botanist who headed the Institutes of Botany and Ecology at the Austral University. The former was jailed several days and then allowed to return to Argentina. The latter was supposed to leave "voluntarily" with a police escort to the international airport of Santiago where he would board a plane for Germany.

The arrested foreign professors, including myself, were detained after being denounced by their colleagues. We were interrogated by the police (the equivalent of the FBI); however, we were never informed of the charges brought against us. Most of us decided to leave Chile "voluntarily" instead of facing a military trial in Santiago with the possible results of incarceration or deportation.

This de jure "voluntary departure" meant deportation from a country to which we had devoted a meaningful part of our professional lives. In my case and in that of Professor Maria Mana, an American citizen, we were informed by her Chilean husband who had had an interview with the chief attorney general (military) of the Province of Valdivia, that we had been denounced by Mauricio Pilleux, then head of the English Department, in which the three of us worked. Prof. Mana's husband stated that I had 96 charges against me. In the present Chilean environment of neighbor denouncing neighbor and worker fellow worker anything goes; it suffices that the denouncer should be of the right and the victim a left sympathizer.

Of the 500 professors of the Austral University of Chile, approximately 100 risk having their contracts terminated prematurely. At the University of Concepcion, cradle and bastion of the Movimiento Izquierda Revolutionario (Movement of the Revolutionary Left), approximately 50 per cent of the faculty will be fired, while in Santiago at the Pedagogical Institute of the University of Chile (45,000 students), the list of unemployed professors will include almost the entirety of the teaching staff. The School of Science at the Santiago campus of the University of Chile will suffer the same fate.

The significance of all this is much more than a mere personal problem for limited groups of specialists. It implies the disappearance of many departments and schools in the Chilean universities which had been established patiently through their own means and efforts in order to reach academic levels of international acceptance. In the case of the Spanish Department of the Austral University of Chile, the purge will inevitably bring about the disappearance of the Masters Program of Hispanic Philology, an important and recent initiative destined to provide instruction at a post graduate level inside Chile and thereby reduce the cultural dependence this country had upon the United States and Europe. This is just a microcosmic example of the tremendous wastefulness on a national scale and the misuse of human, intellectual, and technical resources.

The machine guns on campus, the jack-booted rectors, the dismissals of staff, the absence of a minimum habeas corpus sense of security and the furtive atmosphere engendered by denunciations of straight political accusations mixed together with Socratic charges of perverting the nation's youth and, lowest of all, sexual smears, are fast emptying the universities of sorely needed foreign and national academics, who under previous regimes have had a large hand in building up academically viable groups of specialists.

The only means of modifying, if not reverting, the military "holy war" against the academic community of Chile, which has been aggravated even more so by the decree of September 29th which removed the democratically elected rectors and replaced them with arbitrarily designated military supervisors, is by the determined reaction from the international academic community against the chaos that is being created in Chilean universities. Several foreign universities have exchange programs with the Austral University—the Gottingen University of Germany, the Liverpool University of England, the Bahia Blanca University of Argentina and also the programs of the Bariloche Foundation (Argentina-Chile) and the California-Chile Exchange. These institutions should exercise all the pressure possible to oblige the military generals to reverse their destructive university policy. The authorities of the Inter-American Development Bank should carefully reflect whether there is any justification in continuing the extension of generous monetary loans to Chilean universities, such as the Austral University, for the purchase of materials and equipment, while at the same time this very university permits itself the luxury of firing some of its best professors. In the midst of the present chaos, the continuation of investments by IBD in Chilean universities seems to lack any economic and academic justification.

The Jewish Community of Chile Under Allende

MORTON M. ROSENTHAL

This article, first published in the January 22, 1971 issue of the Jewish journal Sh'ma, *has been somewhat abridged.*

"All of us who left Cuba since the revolution did so because of ideological and economic reasons and not because of anti-Semitism," said Rabbi Dow Rozencwaig, speaking to a *New York Times* reporter in 1969. Since Castro came to power in 1958 nearly 90 per cent of the 11,000 Jews who lived in Cuba before the revolution have left the island to take up residence in the United States and other countries. Speaking to the same reporter, another former member of the Cuban Jewish community recalled that Jews experienced no discrimination in Cuba, enjoyed all civil liberties and had in fact become Cubans; "it was a tragedy to have to abandon the country."

A similar sequence of events began in Chile after the September 4 presidential elections in which the Popular Unity candidate of the Socialist and Communist parties defeated his closest rival in the three-man race by 40,000 votes. Many Chileans were surprised and shaken by the victory of Dr. Salvador Allende, the first Marxist-Leninist to be democratically elected to the presidency of any country.

Stunned disbelief soon gave way to panic in all groups in the country as stock market prices tumbled. People sold what property they could and rushed to exchange their escudos for dollars, jewels and precious metals. Many, traveling on their identity cards, took the first available seats on flights for, Argentina and other countries, while those who did not have the necessary travel documents for themselves or family members queued up at government offices to obtain them.

Despite severe restrictions on the amount of money the travelers could take out of the country—imposed shortly after the election in an effort to halt the outflow of people and capital—flights from Santiago remained full and Chileans filled hotels in Buenos Aires and the Argentine border town of Mendoza. So great was the Chilean refugees' demand for dollars that it strained Argentine foreign currency reserves and prompted discussion of government controls. Best available estimates are that by the end of November approximately forty thousand Chileans left the country, some permanently and others for extended "vacations," with plans to watch developments from a safe distance. Among those who left were approximately 4,000 Jews, about 10 per cent of the nation's Jewish community.

The Reasons for an Exodus

Jews and non-Jews who fled were motivated by common fears. Many decided to get out while the getting was good, fearing that once Allende took power he would prohibit the emigration of professionals, students and young people with skills needed by the country. Cuba had been badly hurt by the "brain drain" and Fidel Castro reportedly advised Allende to guard against a similar situation in Chile. Others left because they envisioned the abolition or diminution of their economic roles and social status under a socialist regime. During the election campaign Allende had clearly announced his intention to nationalize all banks and basic industry, to put stringent controls on import-export business and to extend government influence and control to other areas of the economy; people took him at his word. A third factor causing people to flee was the fear that Chile might become a totalitarian state, and increasingly come under the influence and control of the Soviet Union.

For Chilean Jews there were additional factors uniquely related to their historical experience. The Jewish community of Chile is slightly more than fifty years old, founded by small numbers of Argentine Jews who made their way over the Andes in search of greater opportunity. The overwhelming majority of Chilean Jews are immigrants from Europe, most of whom arrived between 1934 and 1946; 40 per cent German Jews, 50 per cent East European and 10 per cent Sephardim. Consequently, a majority of Chilean Jews had experienced the horrors of the Hitler era, directly or indirectly, and some have also known first-hand the rigors of life in the Communist bloc. Their experience has made them so wary of totalitarianism that many chose to leave Chile at great personal sacrifice rather than run the risk of being trapped if the traditional democratic traditions of the country were scrapped by the new government. When President Allende met with Jewish leaders, he spoke of the Jews who left Chile "driven by the traumatic experiences suffered in the Second World War" and expressed the hope that they would return.

The Threat of Communist Anti-Semitism

The growing influence of the Communist party and the Soviet Union in Chilean affairs was another factor that had unique implications for Jews. The Communist party of Chile, which has an official membership of about 45,000 is known for its discipline and complete support of Soviet policy in all areas—including the Middle East. Although Allende is the leader of the Socialist party, many members of the Communist party were given important posts in the Allende government, positions from which they can attempt to direct government policies along Communist lines. Because the Soviet Union is now the base of a world-wide anti-Zionist campaign which is also an anti-Semitic campaign in which "Zionist" is the code word for Jew, it is to be anticipated that a concerted effort will be made to spread the Soviet hate campaign in Chile. The Arab campaign of anti-Israel propaganda and attacks—10 bombings in eighteen months—has had a disquieting effect upon Chilean Jews. A combined Soviet-Arab effort might make their position untenable.

The impact on the Jewish community of the flight of one-tenth of its members has been far greater than their number might indicate, since many of those who left were the wealthier members of the community who were in positions of leadership and were also the principal source of financial support for Jewish institutions. The Jewish school, which had an enrollment of 1,300 and was the pride of the community, lost many students and teachers and now teeters on the edge of bankruptcy. One of the main synagogues which had brought a young American rabbi to Chile on a three year contract, asked him to return home after he had been in the country less than two weeks because so many members had left that the congregation could not meet its financial obligations. The rabbi of a second synagogue also left the country, leaving only two congregational rabbis to serve all Chilean Jews, and there is no certainty that these rabbis will remain either. Jewish organizations were in such disarray that in the early part of November an emergency meeting was held to assess the status of the Jewish community and plan for its reorganization, and an emergency fund drive for the maintenance of basic communal institutions was undertaken.

Gestures of Hope and Friendship

President Allende has endeavored in various ways to calm fears and reassure members of the Jewish community. Shortly after his election he personally repaid a small loan at the Banco Israelita. In a private meeting with leaders of the Representative Committee, the roof organization, and other major Jewish organizations, Allende assured those assembled that "the community had nothing to fear," his economic policies would be general in character, and in no instance would they be directed against any group or community. He reminded his visitors that he had for many years had very good friends in the Jewish community and would never even dream of any discriminatory measures.

Doubtlessly mindful of Chilean Jewry's fear of his embracing the Soviet anti-Israel line, Allende expressed his admiration for the pioneering spirit of Israel, whose social and economic development he knew very well. The President also granted a forty minute audience to Naftali Feder, a member of the Mapam party in Israel, who had been invited to the inauguration. His highly publicized meeting with Feder had a dual purpose—to reassure Chilean Jewry and thus slow their emigration and also to balance the presence of numerous representatives of Communist governments. In his conversation with Feder, Allende emphatically restated his support of Israel's right to exist and stressed his determination to proceed slowly and democratically in the implementation of his policies at home.

The Prognosis is, As Usual, Uncertain

What of the future? Will the Jews of Chile go the way of Cuban Jewry or will they remain in Chile, adapting themselves to the changed socio-economic order? It seems likely that the small number of Jewish students, intellectuals and professionals from the lower middle class, who actively supported Allende's candidacy will remain in Chile unless forced out by a Polish-type anti-Semitic campaign. Whether the majority of middle class Jews who are entrepreneurs and professionals will stay will depend largely on the government's not adopting the Soviet anti-Israel line, on the maintenance of democratic safeguards and on the ability of the private economic sector to operate.

Allende has persuaded some Chileans, Jews and non-Jews, to return. Based upon Allende's past record, it seems reasonable that if Allende has his way, Chile will not adopt the Soviet line on Israel, the country will remain democratic and the private economic sector will continue to operate. There are, however, grave doubts as to whether the Chilean president will be able to carry out his program in the manner he has outlined.

Right wing extremists sought unsuccessfully to stir up the army and block Allende's election by assassinating the commander of the Chilean army two days before Congress met and formally elected him president. Although the plot failed to bring about military intervention, rightists are continuing to harass the government and now have a militia operating in the interior.

For the time being, forces on the left pose a more serious threat to Allende than those on the right. Should Allende lose control and be reduced to a puppet of revolutionary groups, it is likely that the basic conditions for Jewish security would no longer exist. In that case, large numbers of Jews who have been attempting to adjust to the new realities of Chilean life would decide that the time had come for them to seek haven in Israel or in other countries. The situation would become even more serious if Allende were to resign or die in office.

For the moment, some Jews are returning while others leave and the majority anxiously watch political developments hoping for the best.

La Prensa, August 25, 1973: Chile, Jewish Communism; Russia, Anti-Jewish Communism

Chile has distinguished itself in the course of its glorious history by, among other virtues, racial tolerance. Neither the place of origin, nor the color of the skin, nor language nor religion, were for Chileans a reason for persecution, hostility, let-alone hatred. Indifference, sympathy, and even friendship were our way of behaving.

Thus there came to Chile and generally remained ever after in our territory, English, French, German, Yugoslav, Arab, Jewish—from different Zionist regions—Swiss and Spanish people, who have come. Here they worked, here they made their fortune. Others brought their own (wealth) to invest it in our land, doing well both for themselves and for us. The safety from oppression, the goodness of our climate, the beauty of our nature, the hospitality of our people, our natives, were all decisive in their taking root.

This situation, which, in a delirium of marvelous dreaming patriotism, someone once called a "happy copy of Eden" came to an end beginning in 1970, a fateful year for the history of Chile, which will be remembered as the worst of national catastrophies, to be compared only with the great calamities which history brings to mind: earthquakes, floods, epidemics.

And why?
Because, apart from the spirit of our "Chilean folk," who have overcome so many troubles from nature and from man, we must add the trouble that one cell has brought us, a cell of Jewish and Communist extraction, which has taken over Chile in the miserable hateful alliance of the ill-named Popular Unity. A sect, a cell which has come to fog over for ever the well-earned prestige which so many pure men of National Judaism had earned for themselves. It is a disgrace for them.

Moreover, this sect, this Judeo-Communist cell, has carried on an undercover, hypocritical racial war against another colony which is honest, hard-working, tirelessly working, which has brought enormous benefit to Chile: the Arabs. And we have in Chile a cruel paradox, unique in the world: whereas in the Soviet Union the Jews are persecuted—in other words, where there exists an anti-Jewish Communism—in Chile we have operating against ourselves, the "Chilean folk," a Jewish Communism. The goals of this sect or cell were fixed from the first days of the Popular Unity in the key positions of our economy: monetary, mineral, and manufacturing. Thus there fell under the control of this sect the Central Bank, the Chilean Development Corporation, the copper and iron mines, electricity, the telephone system, and the textile plants . . . wherever there was enough money, wealth, dollars, gold. Equally, they fell on the textile factories, all belonging to Arabs, to families who came with their own money—as we know—to work in this Chile, which had a supreme law, a political constitution of the Republic, which guaranteed them liberty and honor. These were such as the Yarur, Sumar, Sahid, Laban and other families.

On the other hand, which of these directors, vice-presidents, interventors, coadjutors, administrators, councillors, belonging to the Judeo-Communist sect cell, can boast such a life of work?—only bureaucratic positions, international or national, and generally all paid with the hated North American imperialist dollar.

The "Chilean folk" must fix well in their minds the day of final reckoning—not for revenge, but to witness the route of escape that will be taken by those whose names end in VIC, VICH, LEMY, BON and about 50 others. It will be the "gnashing of teeth," as we read in the Bible.

Are You a Jew?

KLAUS MESCHKAT

This is a translation that appeared in the October 4, 1973 edition of the West German publication, Der Stern. It presents the recollections of Klaus Meschkat, who formerly was a sociologist at the

134   *Free University of Berlin and, since March, 1973, a full
          professor at the University of Concepcion, in south-
          central Chile.*

Meschkat just had time to pocket some money, then he
was taken into custody. Meschkat described his experiences as a prisoner to *Stern:* "As soon as I had locked
my apartment, the Carabineros, among them two
superior officers, started to push me with rifle butts and
to abuse me. I was pushed into a bus where I had to
squat on the floor, hands folded behind the head.
Together with four other prisoners I was brought to the
4th precinct.

"When I told them I was a German, I was treated better
than the Chileans. Chileans were beaten and thrashed
repeatedly. I had to give them my name and address,
then I was put into a cell where another 40 people were
squatting; the cell was 2½ to 4 meters large. I had to
spend my first night in prison in a squatting position.

"In the morning, everything we had was taken from us.
Then a guard told us we would be brought to 'the island.'
I had been told by my fellow prisoners that the island was
located north of the military base in Talcahuano, in open
sea. All political prisoners were brought there. The
following morning, in a bus provided by the navy, we
received an envelope with our documents: what was
missing was the money.

"At the Talcahuano base, we were received by navy
cadets armed with wooden clubs. They ferociously beat
everybody who alighted from the bus and yelled: 'Lie
down!' We had to lie on the ground, hands folded behind
our heads, legs crossed. Then they started to torment us.
We had to alternately throw ourselves down and jump
up again. Those who weren't quick enough were beaten
with rifle butts.
"They wore us down with the repeated threat: 'Now it
won't be long before we shoot you.' There was a growing
fear which it was impossible to resist. I firmly expected to
be shot.

"One and a half hours later we were put on a ship that

brought us to the island of Quiriquina. We got off the ship and were brought to the gymnasium of the cadet college. There were already about 200 prisoners—mostly people who knew each other—professors, students and workers whom I had met while doing research. One of my students told me that he had been beaten so savagely for four hours by the Carabineros that he had considered committing suicide.

"Many people from the region of Concepcion had broken ribs. When they took off their bandages one could see that the whole body was blue. They told us they had been beaten with rifle butts, sticks and wet towels. They had not been assaulted during a systematic interrogation, but during the booking procedure.

"After four days on the island I was interrogated for the first time. There was no torturing then. Among other things they wanted to know from me who had been responsible for the leftist propaganda at the university. Then I was to inform against people who had done political work at the institute. After questions of this nature the navy lawyer Acuna suddenly wanted to know: 'Are you a Jew?' That is a question which sticks out in my memory.

"And for the following reasons. We had been approximately 30 foreigners in the camp, among us the Belgian professor Jacques Silberberg, a sociologist. Silberberg is accused of having been an organizer of MIR. However, from his criticism of MIR I know that he was neither a member of, nor sympathetic to, the organization. After a visit by Acuna, he was sent to solitary confinement. It may have been a coincidence that the navy lawyer had asked me whether I was Jewish and sent Silberberg (who was Jewish) into solitary confinement. But it may also be that the anti-semitism which originated in a campaign of the right and the Christian Democrats now plays a role among the officers of the navy, many of whom speak German, come from German families, and have German names.

"Shortly after the visit by a commission of jurists, the discipline in the camp was suddenly tightened. Now barbed wire fences were erected. During the following weeks, many people arrived at the camp—not only from the province of Concepcion, but also from the provinces of Bio-Bio and Nuble—among them the former minister of agriculture, Hidalgo. From the city of Los Angeles, the capital of the province of Bio-Bio, came people who were in a very bad condition. After their arrest they had been forced to remain in a squatting position, hands behind their necks, for 40 hours, without any food. Repeatedly they had been beaten.

"In Los Angeles, it was reported that one officer, whose name was given as Cluss, had given people a special treatment. A socialist deputy named Perez had been brought in. There is a song in Spanish about a mouse named Perez who fell in a pot and squeaked. This lieutenant had forced the deputy Perez to crawl the floor on his hands and feet and imitate the mouse Perez. While being beaten constantly he had to turn around in circles and squeak. The people who told me this had been witnesses to the incident, because the spectacle was produced for his fellow prisoners to watch.

"While I was on the island, it was being transformed into a concentration camp. One day all the prisoners—by now there were about 700—had to line up in groups of 30. We formed groups at random. Units were formed out of the groups of 30. From now on everything happened in unit formation—washing, roll call, drawing rations. Within the units section leaders were appointed who advanced to a liaison position between prisoners. I remember a former officer who suddenly started to give orders. Thus, slowly a hierarchy came into being, similar to the Kapos in the concentration camps of the Nazis. This whole effort of organizing the prisoners, erecting barbed wire fences, and the announcement we would have the opportunity to work on the island, indicates in my opinion that the prisoners have to stay on the island for an extended period of time.

"When I had resigned myself to this situation, one morning my name was called up and I was told that I would be set free. The only condition—I had to leave the country immediately."

German Social Democratic members of parliament had
intervened with the military junta on behalf of the
arrested Germans.

The Cardinal and the Generals

AGOSTINO BONO

This is a slightly edited version of an article which appeared in the October 18, 1973 issue of Latinamerica Press.

Cardinal Raul Silva Henriquez of Santiago has criticized Pope Paul VI for having a distorted image of Chile under the military junta. The statement seems strange, not only for its criticism of the Pope, but also because it comes after the Catholic Bishops Conference issued a declaration listing 65 cases of government persecution against priests and religious. Such a statement could not have been issued without approval of Cardinal Silva, the most powerful church figure in the country.

These seemingly contradictory events· are explained by the cardinal's desire to maintain correct relations with the junta while refusing to give them full recognition. Cardinal Silva, as has been his policy with previous governments, prefers to work behind the scenes to smooth over difficulties.

The difficulties with the military could be legion as Christian social action in Chile is the most advanced in

Latin America, giving rise to a group called Christians for Socialism, containing about 200 members mostly priests, adopting the Marxist analysis of socio-economic reality. This group, plus numerous other Christians sympathetic to the Allende government for non-Marxist reasons are under fire from the military which has adopted a completely reactionary stance toward the overthrown government.

Although Cardinal Silva openly disagreed with the Marxist Christian group, he feels a responsibility for the safety of the members as they remain within the Church and never sought an open split from the institutional structure. He is also deeply worried about the human rights situation, especially regarding the thousands of people still detained by the government.

In his bargaining with the military Cardinal Silva has withheld uncritical support and gave a subtle slight to the new rulers at the Sept. 18 ecumenical prayer service marking Independence Day. The military wanted the service, at which the cardinal gave the homily, as a sign of Church support for the junta. However, the service was only a prayer of thanksgiving instead of the more solemn Te Deum, the service offered at the inauguration ceremonies for Allende. Uncritical support from the Catholic Church is important in Chile where 89 per cent of the population profess Catholicism.

During the sermon, the cardinal offered subtle criticism asking that the examination of the past government be "more inquisitive than condemnatory." He also defended the Christian social action spirit.

When God stimulates people "to evangelize the poor and liberate the oppressed, He certainly is not asking us to negate or destroy the soul of Chile," he emphasized.

Cardinal Silva's chastisement of the Pope came immediately after a closed door meeting with the junta. Apparently, the Pope's declarations that the junta's executions are "irrational and inhumane" came as a bomb shell, destroying the cardinal's credibility with the military. He said the Pope's information did not come from the "regular channels," meaning the episcopacy.

The cardinal's approach has been a gradual escalation of public criticism in relation to junta willingness to compromise. The meeting preceding Cardinal Silva's criticism of the Pope came after the bishops conference released the information about persecution of Church people.

The cardinal's quick retort to the Pope could also be a message to the Vatican to replace the current apostolic nuncio, Archbishop Sotero Sanz Villalba. Archbishop Villalba was appointed after Allende's election for the purposes of establishing good relations with the Marxist government. The previous nuncio was considered sympathetic to the Christian Democrat government of Eduardo Frei. Now that Allende is dead, the cardinal may be telling the Vatican to send someone else if the Pope is basing his statements on information from the current nuncio.

In any case, the cardinal's criticism does not mean a lack of deep worry over the current Chilean situation. It reflects more the desire to follow a fixed strategy of correct but cool relations rather than open confrontation. However, if the junta continues its repressive policy, it could mean an open break. This would give rise to a situation similar to those in Paraguay and Brazil where the Catholic Church becomes the only public institution able to effectively oppose the government.

Neither side wishes that in Chile. Everything depends on whether the junta compromises before the bishops escalate beyond the point of no return.

The Clerical Toll

The following account of Catholic priests who have been killed, expelled or have taken asylum appeared in the October 18, 1973 issue of the church-related publication Latinamerica Press, *published in Lima.*

Weeks after the September 11 *coup d'etat* in Chile, the Press still has not had full access to official data, and perhaps the real total number of persons who have fallen will never be known, from the "suicide" of President Salvador Allende to the number of "missing."

Regarding the clergy, an incomplete list shows the following victims:

At least four French priests expelled from Chile: Pierre Dupuy, of Valparaiso (his Bishop Emilio Tagle had reportedly threatened him with suspension before the coup); Roberto Lebeque, who worked in the National Shrine of Maipu; Mauricio Dutaur, pastor of Paillaco; and one or two more as yet unidentified from Rancagua.

Four French priests have sought asylum in their Embassy and await safe-conduct passes to leave Chile: Carlos Condamin, from Talca; Andre Meutle, from Puerto Montt; Ives, who worked in the Barrancas hospital; Pierre Lavallois, from the Concepcion diocese.

Three French priests were outside Chile on September 11 and cannot return: Father Dubois, of Concepcion; Guido Lebret, of Talca, who worked to rehabilitate prostitutes; and Rene Louvel of Osorno.

Several Canadian Oblate priests, numbering four or five altogether, raise to over a dozen the number of progressive foreign priests expelled from Chile in the first month of the military regime. A U.S. missionary Brother and seminarian were held under arrest for 11 days in the national stadium, then expelled.

Standing alone was the case of the Spanish priest Juan Alsina. He had been the Vicar Cooperator in Barrancas, San Antonio, and was assassinated along with some other extremists in Santiago's San Juan de Dios Hospital, where he worked as an employee.

Father Alsina's corpse was found in the Mapocho River three days after he was shot. Some days later more than 40 priests headed by the Bishops' Vicar concelebrated Mass in his memory.

New York Times, November 7, 1973: Chilean Cleric Sees Marxism Coexisting with Latin Church.

The Roman Catholic Archbishop of Santiago, Chile, was quoted today as having said that he hoped it would be possible that Marxism and Christianity could coexist in a Latin-American society.

The Catholic News Agency said that the Archbishop, Raul Cardinal Silva Henriquez, made the statement in

142 replying to a question at a meeting of the Salesian Order in Rome last week.

"Answering this question," the Cardinal said, "I would have to make a prophecy, but I am not a prophet. I hope it will be possible. In Latin America, socialism without Christian elements is not possible."

The Cardinal did not mention any nation. The Chilean military overthrew the Marxist government of President Salvador Allende Gossens on Sept. 11.

Letter Sent to Junta

The agency said that before leaving Chile, the Cardinal "sent a letter to the military junta to try to get them to stop the summary executions and to not deprive the workers of the social gains they had achieved in the preceding regime."

The agency reported that the Cardinal called President Allende "an idealist, a romantic of socialism who did not keep around him men able to translate the ideas into practical, economic, or social means."

"Allende tried to effect a proletariat dictatorship on a large scale," he said, "but he left the church an effective freedom. We were confident in his promise in respect to the church because Allende listened to us."

THE POLITICS OF INTERVENTION

In this section we investigate the nature and extent of U.S. political involvement in the overthrow of the Chilean government. (In the next section the question of financial involvement in Chile is viewed.) Our first presentation is a statement made by Senator Kennedy on the Senate floor two days after the coup. After lamenting the death of President Allende he raises the question of a direct U.S. role, if any, and a review of this nation's past affronts to the Chilean President. He calls upon the new Secretary of State to testify in open session in order to clarify matters. Following, there is the transcript of a Senate speech by Senator Abourezk that goes more deeply into a matter that was touched upon in our previous document—the status of the more than 10,000 political refugees in the nation who had sought asylum during the Frei and Allende presidencies. This community was being particularly hard hit by the policies of the new military junta. Mr. Kubisch, the new head of the Bureau of Inter-American Affairs of the Department of State, next comments on this alleged U.S. role and promptly denies it. (His claims that "there were no embargoes or restrictions placed on trade with Chile" are challenged in the next

144   *section.) After this, Tad Szulc, in his*
        Washington Post *article, strongly suggests*
        that while the CIA's exact role in the over-
        throw of Allende is still unclear, it has
        traditionally been involved in Chilean politics
        past and present, according to the secret tes-
        timony of the agency's director which the ar-
        ticle reveals. Our last selection is a letter from
        Prof. Richard R. Fagen to Senator Fulbright
        which raises disturbing questions concerning
        the role of the U.S. Embassy in Santiago
        during the period immediately after the coup:
        its failure to adequately defend the safety of
        U.S. citizens, and in particular the conduct of
        Frederick Purdy, the Chief Consul at the
        Embassy. The charges made against Purdy
        were strengthened by two articles sub-
        sequently published in the **New York Times**
        on November 20, 1973.

Senator Edward Kennedy on the Fall of Allende

The following statement was made by Mr. Kennedy on the floor of the Senate, September 13, 1973.

Mr. President: I expressed my deep regret and concern yesterday at the tragedy unfolding in Chile where the overthrow of a democratically elected government is taking place. Whatever our personal views of the policies being undertaken by the government of President Allende, the overriding fact is that he was elected by a vote of the people of Chile. To see Chile take its place alongside other nations whose political course has been determined by military action is particularly tragic since this nation had rightly prided itself on its democratic ideals and on the adherence of its military to constitutional principles.

Now we learn of the death of President Allende. I can only express my deep condolences to the family, friends and supporters of this man. At this moment, whether he was a Marxist or not makes little difference. He believed passionately in his own philosophy and he worked within the democratic system to try to effect programs to carry out that philosophy.

His death during this violence cannot be seen with anything but sorrow by any man who treasures the principle that political decisions should be made through the use of ballots rather than bullets.

We can only hope that in Chile there will be the most rapid return to the rule of law.

We also hope that the new government will protect the rights of thousands of political refugees who have fled to Chile from other countries. Because of disturbing reports that have reached us about their safety, yesterday I cabled the High Commissioner for Refugees to solicit his attention and concern.

Already in the press, there is speculation about the role of the U.S. government in this incident as a result of past actions of this Administration. The State Department has acknowledged it was aware of such reports. However, the White House has denied that information was communicated to the President. There is no reason to doubt those statements.

However, to dispel any doubts, I would hope that the Senate Foreign Relations Committee would resolve any suspicions by requesting the nominee for Secretary of State, Mr. Kissinger, to testify directly on this matter in public session.

I expressed my own concern about our policy toward Chile in October 1971, a year after President Allende took office. In a speech to the Chicago Council on Foreign Relations, I stated:

> The election of a Marxist president in Chile ushered in a period of great delicacy as thoughtful men of both nations groped to find the path of accommodation.

> A wise Administration policy would have recognized that the Chilean experiment in socialism had been decided by the people of Chile in an election far more democratic than the charade we saw last week in Vietnam.

> But the Administration response was brusque and frigid, colored by its attachment to the ideology of the cold war. We can never know whether a more sensitive policy toward Chile might have helped to avoid the expropriation decision, which we learned of today.

> President Nixon decided not to send the traditional note of congratulations to the Chilean President on his election.

> The White House snubbed a personal invitation from President Allende for the U.S. Carrier Enterterprise to dock in Valparaiso, after Admiral Zumwalt's acceptance had been widely and favorably publicized in Chilean newspapapers.

> The Administration blocked Export-Import Bank financing of jets for Chile's national airlines as a way of publicly pressuring Chile to reach a satisfactory solution of the copper controversy. Now we find the government of Chile negotiating with the Soviet Union for those jets.

> Similar heavy-handed policies have been used by this country in the Inter-American Development Bank and

other multilateral lending organizations. The multilateral aim is to depoliticize development assistance and it is a perversion to twist those institutions into being exponents of U.S. foreign policies.

The revelations of the ITT affair, so ably described by the Senate Subcommittee on Multilateral Corporations, also lays out the history of our actions. Those actions inevitably contributed—in however marginal a way—to the economic difficulties experienced by the Allende government.

I would hope that a thorough re-examination of this policy would be part of any review into the current tragedy.

Senator James Abourezk on the Fate of Foreign Refugees Residing in Chile

Mr. Abourezk presented his statement to the U.S. Senate on September 22, 1973.

Mr. President, I am deeply concerned over the unfortunate events that have taken place—and are occurring at this moment—in Chile. Chile has had for many years the most advanced and stable democracy in South America. With few exceptions its republican institutions have been respected since independence.

In addition to its political stability, Chile has had a longtime tradition of granting political asylum to those persecuted for political reasons.

For these two reasons, Chile has always been recognized as a political oasis in a continent plagued with dictatorial regimes. There are between 10 and 13 thousand exiles now in Chile. The largest number are Bolivians—4,000—followed closely by Brazilians and Uruguayans—each with 3,000. The remainder—2,000 to 3,000—are from a number of other Latin American countries.

Many of these people, including 2,000 Brazilians, came to Chile in 1964 prior to the Allende government and were warmly received by the then President Frei and the Christian Democratic government. Even before that time the country had received exiles from such countries as Haiti, Cuba, the Dominican Republic, Panama, and Peru, many of whom still reside in Chile.

The recent military coup against the constitutional government of Chile has prompted many respected religious leaders, scholars, statesmen, and journalists from around the world to express grave concern for the well-being of these exiles and those Chilean supporters of the constitutional government who have refused to submit to the military junta.

News reports—despite military censorship—and junta communiques have provoked increasing alarm. It has been reported by a variety of news sources that killings have already exceeded 5,000 and that many thousands more are being held prisoners. Junta communiques have sought to make the political exiles the scapegoat for Chile's internal problems. To justify their coup the generals have fabricated plots supposedly hatched by the exile community. They have even stated that their political exiles face forced return to their home countries which surely would be to send them to prison, torture, and execution.

The influence of the American government and public opinion is of utmost importance in the course of events in Chile. Many of the Chilean military have been trained by the U.S. government. The United States has in recent years doubled aid to Chile's military while cutting off all economic aid to Chile's civilian economy. U.S. involvement in plots to block the election of Dr. Allende, in

ITT maneuverings and in an all-out economic squeeze on the Allende government are well known. Whether or not we agreed with his policies is not the issue here. We cannot disassociate ourselves from the bloodshed in Chile and especially from the plight of the foreign political exiles and Chilean nationals so urgently in need of asylum.

Whether or not we agreed with Allende's policies is now irrelevant. He was chosen by constitutional means and overthrown by unconstitutional force and violence. The military junta, like its twins in Brazil and Uruguay, blames foreigners for the trouble. These foreigners now face deportation or worse. If sent back to Bolivia, Brazil, Uruguay, Paraguay or the other dictatorships, these people face death or prison.

Let us return to a former image of American support for oppressed people; let us return to our historical conscience and offer assistance to all the political refugees, and let us protest to our own State Department and to the military junta leaders to end the repression. We have helped to cause this situation. We must now act to at least try to save as many people as possible.

The United States is Innocent of Complicity

The following statement was made by Mr. Kubisch before the Sub-Committee for Inter-American Affairs of the House of Representatives on September 20, 1973.

I am very happy to appear before this Committee today and discuss recent events in Chile and United States policy. I am prepared to give you a brief summary of the current situation in Chile as we understand it, although I assume that most of the members present have a good idea of the general conditions in the country now and events leading up to the coup.

However, perhaps I should take this opportunity at the outset to comment on false charges from some quarters that the United States government had advance knowledge of or participated in some way in the overthrow and death of President Allende.

Gentlemen, I wish to state as flatly and as categorically as I possibly can that we did not have advance knowledge of the coup that took place on September 11. In the light of what I consider to be some rather imprecise reporting on the matter, I want to distinguish between our receiving reports about the *possibility* of a coup in Chile and our having advance *knowledge* that a coup would take place.

The facts are that we had received many reports over a long period of time about the possibility of a coup in Chile. Such reports and speculations were rife in Chile itself. Indeed, President Allende himself had commented publicly about them and there was even a report in a Santiago daily newspaper on September 11 that a coup by the Chilean Armed Forces was scheduled for that very day.

All of the earlier reports that had speculated about or predicted coup attempts turned out to be false except the last one, which was received in our offices Tuesday morning, September 11 after the coup had already begun.

However, there was no contact whatsoever by the organizers and leaders of the coup directly with us and we did not have definite knowledge of it in advance.

In a similar vein, either explicitly or implicitly, the United States government has been charged with involvement or complicity in the coup. This is absolutely false. As official spokesmen of the United States government have stated repeatedly, we were not involved in the coup in any way.

I would at this point like to comment also on the subject of United States-Chile economic relations during the past several years.

In my opinion, the position of the United States government was quite correct and fully understandable. The United States had no desire to provoke a confrontation with the Allende government. On the contrary, strong efforts were repeatedly made to seek ways to resolve our differences, although there were expropriations without compensation by the Chilean government of over $700 million of American private investment during this period. In addition, Chile defaulted on over $100 million in debt to the United States government in the same period.

The facts are that there were no embargoes or restrictions placed on trade with Chile. United States firms continued to be major suppliers of food, parts and equipment for the Chilean economy. Bilaterally, we continued a variety of programs, such as A.I.D. people-to-people activities, Food for Peace assistance, the Peace Corps, and scientific and cultural exchanges. We continued to disburse normally on the remaining A.I.D. loans after Dr. Allende ascended to office. While there were no new bilateral development loans, it should be noted that we had cut back sharply on A.I.D. development lending in Latin America, including Chile, even before the Allende government took office. In any case, the Chilean government did not request any new development loans.

In the international field, multilateral banks continued to disburse existing loans to Chile totalling $83 million from August 1971-August 1973, this sum representing an increase in annual disbursements as compared with the three years prior to Dr. Allende's coming to power.

However, the economic policies themselves that were pursued by the Allende government resulted in the steadily deteriorating economic situation. The un-willingness of the government to modify its policies made it inevitable that international lending agencies would curtail their programs for Chile and, in any case, the United States could not have voted favorably for some of this assistance because of legal restrictions.

The Paris Club, consisting of various creditor nations, concluded there was little that could be done for Chile unless the government adopted policies they could support. I repeat, however, that it was not the United States, but the institutions, themselves, which made their decisions.

In sum it is untrue to say that the United States government was responsible—either directly or in-directly—for the overthrow of the Allende regime.

Much concern has naturally been shown for the human tragedy that has resulted from recent events in Chile. The American people and their government have traditionally demonstrated such concern for the suffering of others throughout the world. The United States has given active support in numerous ways to alleviating suffering and furthering the respect of human rights. With regard to Chile, we have already expressed regret at the loss of human lives and at the death of President Allende.

We have also been concerned with reports of violations of human rights in Chile. However, to my knowledge, many of these reports are unsubstantiated and not necessarily indicative of the policies to be followed by the new government of Chile once the situation there has fully stabilized.

Moreover, I understand that the Chilean authorities have already given the U.N. Human Rights Commission assurances with regard to the refugees in that country.

Mr. Chairman, Members of the Committee, in closing I would like to emphasize once again that the situation in Chile is an evolving one. As the new government begins to set out its economic, social and other policies, we will endeavor to formulate our own policies to respond to the realities of the new situation.

We were not responsible for the difficulties in which Chile found itself, and it is not for us to judge what would have been best or will now be best for the Chilean people.

That is for Chileans themselves to decide, and we respect their right to do this. If in the tasks that face them now, we can be of help, and if our help is wanted by Chile, I am sure we will do our best to provide it in the spirit of understanding and friendship that the American people have long felt for the people of Chile.

The CIA and Chile

TAD SZULC

The following article, entitled "The View from Langley," first appeared in the October 21, 1973 issue of The Washington Post.

Was the United States, through the Central Intelligence Agency or otherwise, directly involved in the events that led to the bloody coup d'etat in Chile last Sept. 11?

Actual involvement in the military revolution that ousted the late President Salvador Allende Gossens, a Socialist, has been roundly denied by the Nixon administration and the CIA in particular. But given the CIA's track record in overthrowing or attempting to overthrow foreign governments—Iran, Guatemala, the Bay of Pigs,

154   Laos and so on—deep suspicions have persisted that the agency, operating under White House directives, has been much more than an innocent observer of the Chilean scene since Allende's election in 1970.

Ten days ago, the CIA rather surprisingly if most reluctantly, went quite a way to confirm many of these suspicions. It did so in secret testimony on Oct. 11 before the House Subcommittee on Inter-American Affairs by its director, William E. Colby, and Frederick Dixon Davis, a senior official in the agency's Office of Current Intelligence. The transcript of the testimony was made available to this writer by sources in the intelligence community.

This extensive testimony touches principally on the CIA's own and very extensive covert role in Chilean politics, but it also helps in understanding and reconstructing the administration's basic policy of bringing about Allende's fall one way or another.

We are apprised not only that the CIA's estimate of the number of victims of the military government's repression is four times the official Santiago figures but that the United States, in effect, condones mass executions and imprisonments in Chile because a civil war there remains "a real possibility." Yet, even Colby warned that the junta may "overdo" repression.
Colby's and Davis' testimony, in parts unclear and contradictory, offered a picture of the CIA's activities in Chile between Allende's election in 1970 and the Sept. 11 coup ranging from the "penetration" of all the major Chilean political parties, support for anti-regime demonstrations and financing of the opposition press and other groups to heretofore unsuspected Agency involvement in financial negotiations between Washington and Santiago in late 1972 and early 1973 when the Chileans were desperately seeking an accommodation.

There are indications that the CIA, acting on the basis of its own reports on the "deterioration" of the Chilean economic situation, was among the agencies counseling the White House to rebuff Allende's attempts to work out a settlement on the compensations to be paid for nationalized American property and a renegotiation of Chile's $1.7 billion debt to the United States.

A No-Help Policy

Actually, the basic U.S. posture toward Allende was set forth by Henry A. Kissinger, then the White House special assistant for national security affairs, at a background briefing for the press in Chicago on Sept. 16, 1970, 12 days after Allende won a plurality in the elections and awaited a run-off vote in Congress. Kissinger said then that if Allende were confirmed, a Communist regime would emerge in Chile and that Argentina, Bolivia and Peru might follow this example.

For the next three years, the U.S. policy developed along two principal lines. One was the denial of all credits to the Allende government—Washington even blocked loans by international institutions—to aggravate Chile's economic situation when Allende himself was bogging down in vast mismanagement of his own. The other line was the supportive CIA activity to accelerate the economic crisis and thereby encourage domestic opposition to Allende's Marxist Popular Unity government coalition.

The only exception to the ban on credits was the sale of military equipment to the Chilean armed forces—including the decision last June 5 to sell Chile F-5E jet fighter planes—presumably to signal United States support for the military. Colby's testimony as well as other information showed that the United States had maintained close contacts with the Chilean military after Allende's election.

The Nixon administration's firm refusal to help Chile, even on humanitarian grounds, was emphasized about a week before the military coup when it turned down Santiago's request for credits to buy 300,000 tons of wheat here at a time when the Chileans had run out of foreign currency and bread shortages were developing.

On Oct. 5, however, the new military junta was granted

$24.5 million in wheat credits after the White House overruled State Department objections. The department's Bureau of Inter-American Affairs reportedly believed that such a gesture was premature and could be politically embarrassing.

An "Unfortunate" Coup

Paradoxically, Washington had not hoped for the kind of bloody military takeover that occurred on Sept. 11. For political reasons, it preferred a gradual destruction from within of the Chilean economy so that the Allende regime would collapse of its own weight. The CIA's role, it appeared, was to help quicken this process.

Under questioning by Rep. Michael J. Harrington (D-Mass.), Colby thus testified that the CIA's "appreciation" of the Chilean economy was that "it was on a declining plane on the economic ground in terms of internal economic problems—inflation, with 320 per cent inflation in one year, the closure of the copper mines, and so forth, your total foreign deficit was more than the need for it. They couldn't import the food because their deficit was such that over the long term they had no base for it." Elsewhere in his testimony, Colby said that the CIA reported "accurately an overall assessment of deterioration" and that with the Chilean navy pushing for a coup, it was only a question of time before it came.

But Colby also told the subcommittee that "our assessment was it might be unfortunate if a coup took place. The National Security Council policy was that it is consistent with the feeling it is not in the United States interest to promote it." He made this comment after Rep. Charles W. Whalen (R-Ohio) asked Colby whether he agreed with earlier testimony by Jack Kubisch, the assistant secretary of state for Inter-American affairs, that the administration believed that "it would be adverse to our own United States interest if the government of Chile were overthrown."

This theme was further developed in a letter on Oct. 8 from Richard A. Fagen, professor of political science at Stanford University, to Sen. William Fulbright, chairman of the Senate Foreign Relations Committee, reporting on a meeting between Kubisch and a group of scholars representing the Latin American Studies Association.

Fagen said that Kubisch took the view that "it was not in our interest to have the military take over in Chile. It would have been better had Allende served his entire term taking the nation and the Chilean people into complete and total ruin. Only then would the full discrediting of socialism have taken place. Only then would people have gotten the message that socialism doesn't work. What has happened has confused this lesson."

"No Indication" of Support

Colby's testimony on the CIA's activities in Chile supplied a considerable amount of new information, some of it contradictory, under vigorous questioning by the subcommittee.

Thus at one point Colby said that "I can make a clear statement that certainly CIA had no connection with the coup itself, with the military coup. We didn't support it, we didn't stimulate it, we didn't bring it about in any way. We obviously had some intelligence coverage over the various moves being made but we were quite meticulous in making sure there was no indication of encouragement from our side."

Colby also insisted that the CIA was not involved with the prolonged strike by Chilean truckers that preceded the coup.

But pressed by Rep. Harrington, Colby acknowledged that the CIA may have assisted certain anti-Allende demonstrations. The following discussion ensued:

> HARRINGTON: Did the CIA, directly or indirectly, assist these demonstrations through the use of subsidiaries of United States corporations in Brazil or other Latin American countries?

> COLBY: I think I have said that the CIA did not assist the trucking strike.

HARRINGTON: I think it's a broader, and more intentionally broader, question—any of the demonstrations that are referred to in the course of this questioning.

COLBY: I am not quite sure of the scope of that question.

HARRINGTON: I make specific reference to two, one in the October period of 1972 and one in March of 1973.

COLBY: I would rather not answer the question than give you an assurance and be wrong, frankly. I would rather not. If we did, I don't want to be in a position of saying we didn't. But if we didn't, I really don't mind saying I won't reply because it doesn't hurt. But I don't want to be in a position of giving you a false answer. Therefore, I think I better just not answer that, although I frankly don't know the answer to that question right here as I sit here.

"A Covert Operation"

Though Colby consistently refused to tell the subcommittee whether the CIA's operations in Chile had been authorized by the "40 Committee," the top secret group headed by Kissinger in the National Security Council that approves clandestine intelligence operations, he admitted that "we have had . . . various relationships over the years in Chile with various groups. In some cases this was approved by the National Security Council and it has meant some assistance to them. That has not fallen into the category we are talking about here—the turbulence or the military coup."

In previous testimony before a Senate subcommittee, former CIA Director Richard Helms disclosed that the CIA had earmarked $400,000 to support anti-Allende news media shortly before his election. This was authorized by the "40 Committee" at a meeting in June, 1970. Colby, however, refused to say whether this effort was subsequently maintained, claiming that the secrecy of CIA operations had to be protected. He then became engaged in this exchange with Harrington:

COLBY: That does go precisely on to what we were

operating and what our operations were. I would prefer to leave that out of this particular report. . . .

HARRINGTON: I think we have run exactly into what makes this a purposeless kind of exercise . . .

COLBY: If I might comment, the presumption under which we conduct this type of operation is that it is a covert operation and that the United States hand is not to show. For that reason we in the executive branch restrict any knowledge of this type of operation very severely and conduct procedures so that very few people learn of any type of operation of this nature.

HARRINGTON: And we end up with a situation such as at Sept. 11 because you have a cozy arrangement.

Corporate Cooperation

On the question of support to anti-Allende forces by United States or Brazilian corporations, Colby and Davis gave equivocal answers to the subcommittee. Colby said, "I am not sure." Davis said, "I have no evidence as to that," but Colby interrupted him to remark that "I wouldn't exclude it. Frankly, I don't know of any. However, I could not say it didn't happen."

Subcommittee members pursued at some length the possible involvement by American corporations in the Chilean coup because of previous disclosures that the International Telephone and Telegraph Corp. had offered the CIA $1 million in 1970 to prevent Allende's election and subsequently proposed a detailed plan to plunge Chile into economic chaos.

Rep. Dante B. Fascell (D-Fla.), the subcommittee chairman, raised the question of involvement by Brazilian or other Latin American corporations, many of them subsidiaries of United States firms, because of reports that the anti-Allende moves were widely coordinated. Speaking for the CIA, Davis replied:

There is some evidence of cooperation between business groups in Brazil and Chile. However, this is a small share of the financial support. Most of the support was internal. There is some funding and cooperation among groups with similar outlooks in other Latin American countries. This is true with regard to most of these governments . . . I was not thinking so much of companies or firms so much as groups, organizations of businessmen, chambers of commerce, and that kind of thing in a country such as Brazil.

Discussing the CIA's intelligence operations in Chile, Colby said he "would assume" that the Agency had contacts with Chileans opposed to Allende. Asked by Harrington whether the CIA maintained such contacts in social contexts, Colby said:

If a gentleman talks to us under the assurance he will not be revealed, which can be dangerous in some countries, it would have been very dangerous for those in Chile . . . the protection of that relationship, fiduciary relationship with the individual, requires that I be very restrictive of that kind of information."

Then the following dialogue developed:

FASCELL: Is it reasonable to assume that the Agency has penetrated all of the political parties in Chile?

COLBY: I wish I could say yes. I cannot assure you all, because we get into some splinters.

FASCELL: Major?

COLBY: I think we have an intelligence cover of most of them. Let's put it that way.

FASCELL: Is that standard operating procedure?

COLBY: It depends on the country. For a country of the importance of Chile to the United States' decision-making, we would try to get an inside picture of what is going on there. I can think of a lot of countries where we really don't spend much time worrying about their political parties. I spend much of my time worrying about penetrating the Communist Party of the Soviet Union.

The Economic Role

One of the most intriguing disclosures made by Colby in

his testimony was that the CIA is actively engaged in economic negotiations between the United States and foreign countries. This has not been generally known here, but Colby told the subcommittee that "we would normally contribute to (a) negotiating team."

He said that "we would try to provide them intelligence as backdrop for their negotiations and sometimes help them with appreciation of the problem . . . We follow the day-to-day progress in negotiations. If it's an important economic negotiation, like (Treasury) Secretary Shultz over in Nairobi and places like that, we would be informed of what they are doing and try to help them."

In the context of the Chilean-American negotiations before the coup, the CIA's Davis said that "we did have some quite reliable reporting at the time indicating that the Russians were advising Allende to put his relations with the United States in order, if not to settle compensation, at least to reach some sort of accommodation which would ease the strain between the two countries. There were reports indicating that, unlike the Cubans, they were in effect trying to move Allende toward a compromise agreement. . . . It was our judgment that the (Chileans) were interested in working out some kind of *modus vivendi* without, however, retreating substantially from their position."

Davis added that "our intelligence requirement in the negotiations between the United States and Chile would be to try to find out, through our sources, what their reactions to a negotiating session were, what their reading of our position was, what their assessment of the state of negotiations is."

In his narration of the events leading to the coup, Colby said that "under the general deterioration, it was only a matter of getting the army, the navy and the air force to cover it. Eventually they did get them all in." Colby then compared the Chilean coup to the 1967 Indonesian revolution, reputedly assisted by the CIA, when the army ousted President Sukarno. He said the CIA shared the suspicions of the Chilean military that Allende was planning a coup of his own on Sept. 19 to neutralize the armed forces, but said the CIA had no firm information confirming these suspicions.

"Concern Over Security"

Throughout his testimony, Colby drew a grim picture of the junta's repression and, in effect, predicted that it would worsen even more because of the continued strength of the Chilean left. His estimates of the death toll were roughly four times the figures announced by the junta and he told the subcommittee that the Chilean military had a list of the "most wanted" Allende followers whom they hoped to find and possibly execute.

"Communist Party chief Luis Corvalan is being or will be tried for treason. He may well be sentenced to death regardless of the effect on international opinion," Colby said. This information led to this exchange:

WHALEN: You mentioned those being accused of treason. Did these allegedly treasonable activities occur after the takeover by the military?

COLBY: I think what I referred to was the head of the Communist Party who would probably be tried for treason.

He would probably be tried for treason. He would probably be tried for activities prior to the takeover. You can have some question as to how valid that is in a constitutional legal sense. There have been some who have been accused of it since the takeover.

WHALEN: That confuses me. If he is tried for treason against a government (he) supported, I cannot understand that.

COLBY: You are right.

This was Colby's assessment of the present situation:

Armed opposition now appears to be confined to sporadic, isolated attacks on security forces, but the regime believes that the left is regrouping for coordinated sabotage and guerrilla activity. The government probably is right in believing that its opponents have not been fully neutralized. Our reports indicate that the extremist movements of the Revolutionary Left believes its assets have not been damaged beyond repair. It wants to launch anti-government activity as soon as practical and is working to form a united front of leftist opposition parties. Other leftist groups, including the Communist and Socialist parties, are in disarray, but they have not been destroyed. Exiled supporters of the ousted government are organizing abroad, namely in Rome.

Colby told the subcommittee that "concern over security undoubtedly is what accounts for the junta's continued use of harsh measures to deal with the dissidents. The military leaders apparently are willing to alienate some support at home and endure a bad press abroad, in order to consolidate their hold on the country and finish the job of rooting out Marxist influence."

Chance of "Civil War"

Armed resisters continue to be executed where they are found, and a number of prisoners have been shot, supposedly while "trying to escape." Such deaths probably number 200 or more . . . Several thousand people remain under arrest, including high-ranking officials of the Allende government.

Answering questions, Colby agreed that the CIA's figure of more than 200 executions was higher than the junta's official estimate. He added that "there were a couple thousand, at least, killed during the fighting which surrounded the coup. It is quite possible that if you went to a city morgue you would find that number. The official figure of total killed is 476 civilians and 37 troops to a total of 513. We would guess, we would estimate, it is between 2,000 and 3,000 killed during the struggles. That would not be in my classification as execution . . . Some of those were shot down. There is no question about that. They are not just bystanders . . ."

Colby disagreed, however, with Rep. Robert H. Steele (R-Conn.) that the junta killings have "done no one any good."

"I think our appreciation is that it does them some good . . . The junta, their concern is whether they could take this action of taking over the government and not generate a real civil war, which was the real chance because the Allende supporters were fairly activist. There were armies in the country. There was at least a good chance of a real civil war occurring as a result of this coup," Colby said.

Asked whether civil war remained a possibility, Colby replied that, "It was. It's obviously declining, but it was a real possibility. Yes, I think it is a real possibility. Whether it's a certainty or not is not at all sure."

An Accusation Against the American Embassy in Santiago

Mr. Fagen is a professor of political studies at Stanford University and is president-elect of the Latin American Studies Association. The following letter was sent to Senator J. William Fulbright, the chairman of the Foreign Relations Committee of the U.S. Senate.

Dear Senator Fulbright:

The full scale of the tragedy in Chile is just now coming into focus. Not only have democracy and constitutionalism been destroyed in the name of "saving the nation," but the human costs are unprecedented in the recent history of Latin America. While the military junta inches the body count up from an original 95 to several hundred, all other sources place the figure high in the thousands. John Barnes, an eye-witness reporter for *Newsweek* magazine (October 8) reports that the Santiago morgue alone processed 2,796 bodies in the first two weeks after the attack on the presidential palace. Many of the victims were shot at close range under the chin. He reports viewing decapitated bodies, and writes of a multitude of other incidents reminiscent of the butchery usually associated with war-time occupations and search-and-destroy missions. And his is only one of a great number of voices being raised in a worldwide effort to get at the truth of the Chilean situation.

My purpose in writing to you, however, is more limited— although not unrelated to the savagery perpetrated by the military junta. Specifically, I have been a party and a witness to a small slice of the behavior and activities of the U.S. State Department and the U.S. Embassy in Santiago, before, during, and after the recent military coup. As I fit together the pieces of this behavior from my notes and conversations, the picture that emerges is disturbing in the extreme. And my small slice is, I feel, only the tip of an iceberg that extends both horizontally and vertically through our diplomatic and national security apparatuses. Thus, what I offer here is necessarily a very personal fragment, told as simply as possible. Only the Congress, using its full investigatory powers, can begin to assemble the larger picture and begin to call those who are responsible to account.

In January of 1972, I took leave for 18 months from Stanford University where I am a Professor of Political Science. In February of that year, I established residence in Santiago, Chile, where I worked for the next 18 months (until the end of July, 1973) as a full-time social science consultant to the Ford Foundation. During that period, I also taught as a visiting professor at the Latin American Faculty of the Social Sciences (FLACSO), an internationally sponsored graduate training institution specializing in sociology and political science.

While in Santiago, I met a number of young Americans, graduate students and others, who were living and working in the city. These young Americans were all, in varying degrees, sympathetic to the Allende experiment in profound socio-economic transformation by democratic means. Among the group were three men in their 20's, Charles Horman, Frank Teruggi, and David Hathaway. During my last seven months in Santiago, I had occasion to work quite closely with Horman and Hathaway (particularly the former), for I was editing a book to be published in both English and Spanish and the two of them were hired by me as part-time translators. As part of the same project (and also because of my position in the Ford Foundation and my other professional activities), I also had significant and frequent contacts with Teruggi and other members of this loosely structured group of young Americans.

I had not been in Santiago long before it became quite evident that the expressed hostility of the American Embassy toward the Allende government extended to those members of the American community who were known to cooperate, sympathize, or even take a "neutral" stance toward the regime. I repeatedly heard reports of Embassy personnel commenting to other members of the diplomatic and foreign communities that specific individuals (and institutions) were behaving in ways that were "against the best interests" of the United States. Words such as "traitorous," "commie," "fellow traveler" were bandied about in reference to many of my American friends and acquaintances. Even in the Ford Foundation we found it necessary to discuss in a serious fashion the possibility that our professional relations with a number of government agencies and university departments of leftist orientation were being used (and misused) by Embassy personnel to do personal and institutional damage to us. As can be imagined, in this political and intellectual climate, the allegations about and the pressures on the group of young American citizens—who were without the professional and institutional support which we enjoyed—were much more severe.

Throughout much of 1972, there was a notable vacuum of ambassadorial power at the Santiago Embassy. Edward Korry, the Ambassador until the end of 1971, was very suspected because of his open hostility to the government in power. He was subsequently, of course, badly burned by the ITT and CIA disclosures. Nathaniel

Davis, his replacement, arrived at a difficult and delicate moment. For the first several months, his profile was extraordinarily low, both in the American and the local communities. It was clear to all that the effective operative head of the Embassy was Harry Shlaudeman, the Deputy Chief of Mission in Santiago, a "long-timer" in Chile, an important figure in the Dominican affairs of the mid-1960's, and now back in Washington as the top aid to Jack Kubisch, the Assistant Secretary of State for Inter-American Affairs. Even among persons very much opposed to Allende, Shlaudeman was seen as a hard-liner. His opposition to the Chilean government was un-relenting, and he was often cited by persons who knew him as the high Embassy official most single-mindedly hostile to the positions and the activities of those Americans in Santiago who were supportive of the government.

During this same period, I also had a conversation with a career U.S. Foreign Service Officer. In the course of this conversation, the following information was volunteered to me: 1) that Frederick Purdy, Chief Consul of the U.S. Embassy in Santiago was in fact a CIA agent; 2) that other consular personnel at the Embassy were disturbed by this intrusion of the CIA into their section (I was told that the usual Embassy locations of CIA operatives were the political section, communications, and AID—not consular affairs); 3) that there were serious dangers attached to this double assignment, as CIA agent and consul, not the least of which were the "divided loyalties" that might result should the situation in Santiago "deteriorate." My conversation with this career officer was unwitnessed, and I have no concrete proof of Purdy's alleged double role. I was sufficiently alarmed, however, to repeat the conversation immediately and as completely as possible to a trusted and judicious friend.

At the end of July, 1973, I returned to the United States as scheduled, reassumed my professorship at Stanford, and was in California when the first news of the coup was broadcast. Alarmed by the stories that were being reported, I contacted the past, present and future presidents of the Latin American Studies Association (I am vice-president and president-elect) and suggested that we go to Washington to express our concern to Congressional leaders and urge that certain emergency measures be taken to save lives. A brief report of this trip is appended. On our final day in Washington, Tuesday, September 18, we met for one hour with Mr. Jack Kubisch, the Assistant Secretary of State for Inter-American Affairs. At that time, one full week after the coup, Kubisch told us that there was no real reason to doubt the junta's reports of the number of prisoners, deaths, and executions, that he considered the military leaders to be basically "honest" and "good" men, and that his office would help in whatever way possible were we to have further questions or concerns. On returning to California, I made a special point of keeping in touch with Kubisch's office as the special plight of the young Americans mentioned above began to unfold.

On September 23, the *New York Times* carried a story about the arrest by the Chilean military of Charles Horman, one of the young men who had worked for me as a translator. On Monday morning, September 24, I called Kubisch's office for information on Horman and was told that they would check on it. That evening I called a Stanford graduate student doing dissertation research in Santiago, and found that Horman had been arrested on the 17th of September, and that on the evening of the 20th, Frank Teruggi and David Hathaway (who were roommates) had also been arrested after a police search of their apartment had discovered "leftist literature."

Early in the morning on Tuesday, September 25, my wife and I began the search for the families of Teruggi and Hathaway. The Hathaway's were traced through Amherst College (David was a 1972 graduate), and the Teruggi's through friends in Chicago. Before the day was up, I had talked to the Hathaway family, and the friends of Teruggi had contacted his father in Illinois. For both families, this was the first word that they had received of the plight of their sons. Early in the day, I also called Kubisch's office, presenting my information and its sources in as much detail as possible. The office, in turn, implied that this was the first that they had heard of the cases, and they said that they would "get right on them." Subsequently, I was in almost daily phone contact with Kubisch's office for about a week regarding the Horman, Hathaway, and Teruggi cases. During this period I never received any information from that office that I had not either heard beforehand on the radio, read in the newspaper, or received first-hand in one of my several calls to Santiago. (Incidentally, from about the 24th of September on, telephone communication with Santiago became quite easy. By simply stating that it was an emergency call, I never had to wait more than one-half hour to get through).

On Wednesday the 26th, at approximately 5:00 P.M., David Hathaway was released by the Chilean military authorities into the custody of Frederick Purdy. On Tuesday, October 2, a positive identification of Frank Teruggi's body was made in the Santiago morgue (he died from multiple gunshot wounds, including at least two in the head, one of which damaged his face). As of this writing, Charles Horman is still missing. What happened between September 17 when Charles Horman was first arrested and the end of the first week of October is impossible to piece together fully from this vantage point. However, to the extent that I have been able to reconstruct the story (from conversations with Santiago, with David Hathaway, newspaper reports, and other sources), the chronology is something like the following:

September 17: The home of Charles and Joyce Horman is ransacked by the police in Santiago. Charles is seen by neighbors when he is arrested, ostensibly for "possession of leftist literature." Joyce Horman, staying at the home of a friend because of the curfew (and thus not arrested), reports her husband's arrest to the U.S. Embassy the following day.

September 20: At 8:15 in the evening, the police enter the apartment of Frank Teruggi and David Hathaway. The apartment is ransacked, "leftist literature" is found, and the two young men are led away for interrogation, eventually being taken to the National Stadium. A Chilean woman, in the apartment at the time, witnesses the arrests but is not herself taken or harmed.

September 21: The arrests of Teruggi and Hathaway are reported to the U.S. Embassy by their friends (who have been informed by the witnesses). (As a precautionary measure, and as requested by the Embassy, Teruggi had previously registered with the consular service as a U.S. citizen living in Santiago). In their conversations in the Stadium, Teruggi and Hathaway agree that, if released, both or either should go immediately to the U.S. Embassy to ask protection and seek information on the whereabouts of the other. At about 6:00 in the evening, Teruggi is called out of the small group being held together in the improvised cell. This is perceived by Hathaway and others as very unusual since foreigners arrested and held in the Stadium normally spent several days before being called out, interrogated, and (sometimes) released. Teruggi is not returned nor seen alive again by any of his friends.

September 23: The first news of the arrests of Teruggi and Hathaway comes to Fagen in the United States, as described previously.

September 24: The State Department in Washington is informed by Fagen of the arrests of Teruggi and Hathaway. The State Department implies that this is the first information received, and promises to "get right on it." The families of Teruggi and Hathaway are contacted for the first time, as described above.

September 25: Substantial activities and pressures are generated in Washington and elsewhere by the families and friends of Horman, Teruggi, and Hathaway. There are indications that the State Department is beginning to feel this pressure and is moving "more vigorously."

September 26: At approximately 5:00 P.M., David Hathaway, along with a number of other Americans who had been held in the National Stadium, is released into the custody of Frederick Purdy. Purdy asks no questions about their experiences, but expedites the processing of their documents (needed to leave the country). Purdy tells Hathaway that a body brought into the Santiago morgue on Saturday, September 22, had been tentatively identified by the Chilean authorities as that of Frank Teruggi. Purdy claims he was given this information on Monday the 24th, but says he has not visited the morgue, nor has he called on the Santiago friends of Teruggi to make a positive identification.

September 27: Hathaway goes with Purdy to the morgue to attempt an identification of the body. Hathaway notices that the face of the corpse is intact (subsequent accounts emphasize that Teruggi had been shot in the face) and that a prominent scar on Teruggi's ankle could not be found on the corpse. Despite facial similarities, Hathaway is thus unable to make a positive identification.

September 29: Hathaway returns to the United States. The State Department in Washington continues to inform the family and friends of Teruggi only that there are "conflicting" reports on Teruggi's whereabouts. Meanwhile, the military authorites in Santiago continue to insist that Teruggi was "released" on September 21, a claim which they first made earlier in the week according to the State Department.

October 2: Positive identification of Teruggi's body is made in Santiago (confirmed by local dental records and the fingerprints routinely taken and kept on all foreigners by the Chilean authorities when they issue local identification cards). The Teruggi family is notified of the verification by friends of their son who have been in telephone communication with Santiago.

October 3: The Teruggi family is notified by the State Department of their son's death. Joyce Horman reports from Santiago that the U.S. Embassy is being extremely uncooperative in the search for her missing husband, Charles. Among other things, she reports that she had been told by Embassy personnel that "Charles just probably wanted to get away from you."

October 7: Still no news of Charles Horman, arrested on September 17.

172   What is to be made of this one small slice of the larger picture? At the most specific level, there are a host of disquieting questions:

—Was Purdy a CIA agent masquerading as Consul? If so, what are the implications of this double role? If not, why should a career Foreign Service officer go out of his way to tell me so? Was Purdy, as rumored in Santiago during 1972-73, spying on Americans and sharing that information with the Chilean authorities? If so, under orders from whom?

—In the Horman case, but more dramatically in the Teruggi and Hathaway cases, why were the arrests (reported to the Embassy shortly after they occurred) so long in being reported to the State Department in Washington? Or was the State Department lying when four days after the arrests of Hathaway and Teruggi they informed me that it was "news to them"?

—Why were the families of Hathaway and especially Teruggi informed so tardily, and kept informed so poorly throughout this period? Why was action taken in Santiago on these and other cases only after family and This from our "highest public servant" with responsibility for U.S.-Latin American relations! No regret about the coup other than that it interrupted his preferred scenario for Allende's demise. No shame in equating the U.S. national interest with the discrediting and destruction of the socialist experiment in Chile. Not even any sense of the irony that the "discrediting" of Allende's variant of constitutionalist revolution lends cogent support to the argument that profound structural change will come about only through violence and the rejection of democratic practices. Just decades-old cold warriorism, twisted logic, total lack of concern for the Chilean people, and a single-minded commitment to the destruction of "the Chilean way" by the most convincing means possible (which Kubisch correctly reasoned was not by savage military coup).

So much for "hemispheric cooperation," "neutrality," "social justice," "democracy," "non-intervention" and other fine phrases. What really matters to people who think this way is that the hemisphere be made safe for "the American way of life," and this in turn implies that socialist experiments such as the Chilean must be destroyed as convincingly as possible. It is this common mission of destruction which in the final analysis brings together the State Department, the CIA, the Treasury Department, the Defense Department, the White House, ITT, and others—no matter how different their tactics might seem. And given this mission, it follows that human lives and other values become secondary. Chileans don't count, and even Americans don't count for much—especially if they are relatively young and think "wrong thoughts." It is in this context, permeated by a mentality of destruction, that the death of Frank Teruggi, the disappearance of Charles Horman, and the narrow escape of David Hathaway must be placed. That some American officials did not want great quantities of blood to flow in the streets of Chile (for they believed it obscured the "real lesson") does not absolve them of their guilt and complicity in what has happened.

As stated above, I have only a tiny piece of the story. I hope, moreover, that others who have other pieces of the story will also step forward and be heard. But ultimately it is the Congress of the United States in which we place our hopes. After Watergate and Vietnam, there are indications that many of our elected representatives no longer take at face value the pious statements of the executive branch and the national security apparatus. I thus pray that you and your colleagues in Congress will take the initiative and provide both the forum and the muscle necessary to ensure that the larger picture is assembled and made public. Such truth-telling at this time can only further the cause of freedom and justice in the Americas, and furthering that cause would be a fitting memorial to friends applied significant pressure in the United States?

—Why did it take Purdy more than eight days to establish the identity of Teruggi's body, especially since Teruggi was registered with the Embassy, had many friends in Santiago, and had been fingerprinted and

174   registered (as were all resident foreigners) by the Santiago police? How does one explain the bizarre story of David Hathaway being shown a body which seems not to have been that of his dead roommate?

—Is it true that the U.S. Embassy was uncooperative with Joyce Horman? Was she told, as reported, that her missing husband "probably just wanted to get away from you"? If so, is this individual or bureaucratic sadism—or both?

—How many other Americans suffered the indignities and dangers allegedly suffered by the American woman who went to the U.S. Embassy after the coup asking for help and was told to go see the Chilean police? (*New York Times,* September 29, 1973, p. 3).

These and similar questions could be multiplied almost endlessly were we able to draw on a larger pool of witnesses, informants and knowledgeables.

But as ugly and tragic as the answers to these and similar questions might be, there is yet another layer of ugliness. Here the evidential base is necessarily thin at the moment, but the logic is compelling. I personally believe that the role and behavior of Frederick Purdy, the callousness of other Embassy officials, the unrelenting cold-warriorism of Henry Shlaudeman, the bungling (or mendacity) of the State Department, are all of a piece. And this particular piece, in turn, relates to a much larger picture, ultimately involving the Defense Department, the CIA, the Treasury Department, the White House, and many U.S. corporations. Nothing symbolizes the main thread tying together the larger fabric better than a statement made by Assistant Secretary of State Jack Kubisch in the meeting previously described, held in his office on September 18. At that time, Kubisch (without a trace of self consciousness), stated in front of four witnesses his view of the "United States national interest in Chile." What follows is a paraphrase of what he said, taken from my notes, made immediately after the meeting:

It was not in our interest to have the military take over

in Chile. It would have been better had Allende served his entire term, taking the nation and the Chilean people into complete and total ruin. Only then would the full discrediting of socialism have taken place. Only then would people have gotten the message that socialism doesn't work. What has happened (the military takeover and bloodshed) has confused this lesson.

Frank Teruggi and the thousands of others who have died in Chile during the past three weeks.

Very truly yours,
Richard R. Fagen
Professor of Political Science
Stanford University
Stanford, California

cc: Secretary of State Henry Kissinger

Senator Edward Kennedy

Senator Jacob Javits

Senator Gale McGee

Senator Adlai Stevenson

Congressman Dante Fascell

Congressman Donald Fraser

Congressman Paul McCloskey

Mr. David Hathaway

Mr. Frank Teruggi Sr.

Mrs. Joyce Horman

ECONOMIC INTERVENTION

In this section we survey the extent of the policy of economic denial practiced against the Allende government by the United States. This is the theme explored in Mr. Collins' inquiry. One of his conclusions is that economic denial could be considered the central thrust of Washington's policy towards Chile. The second document investigates this nation's attitude toward renegotiating Chile's debt and suggests that the Nixon administration dragged its feet even though Allende had suggested that the question of compensation for the nationalized copper mines should be resolved by conciliation procedures. The next article tells us that the military junta has been far more successful in attracting private loans from U.S. banks than the government which it overthrew. Our last selection announces a $24 million agricultural credit from the United States. Thus, in a matter of weeks, the new government has acquired eight times more agricultural assistance from this country than the Allende government received in its three years of existence.

Tightening the Financial Knot

JOSEPH COLLINS

Mr. Collins is a member of the Institute for Policy Studies in Washington, D.C. The following is an extract from a recently written lengthy memorandum on the broad subject of U.S.-Chilean relations.

The Chilean economy depended on a massive and uninterrupted flow of imports, including over 30 per cent of its food, machinery and machine parts, much of which could only be obtained from the U.S. Chile had only one basic export—copper—and its price on the world market was rapidly tumbling. In addition, Allende's Popular Unity Coalition had inherited from the Alliance for Progress era the world's second highest per capita foreign debt, the bulk of which would soon become due. Finally, Allende's coalition, without the control or cooperation of Congress and with a judiciary and armed forces prejudiced in favor of private ownership and foreign investment, commanded little of the governmental power so obviously essential if external economic warfare was to be resisted internally. Chile was thus a ready-made victim. Since the kind of invisible economic blockade envisioned by the U.S. government's low profile strategy called for basically negative measures, the fascist take-over in Chile might well be the U.S. government's cheapest coup. (Although, as time may show, maintaining the military junta in power might prove a good deal more costly.)

Equally important, low profile economic warfare from a distance had the advantage of being virtually "invisible" to U.S. public opinion. It employed the tools and techniques of international finance, a subject which is seldom discussed and little understood by non-economists. The evening news carries no footage of an invisible economic blockade. Its weapons can be easily disguised as legitimate, "everyday" legal and financial operations. There is virtually no public debate in the United States about the economics of underdeveloped countries, nor about the merits of expropriation and its legal and economic rationale. Low profile economic warfare offers the executive a new and subtle power, far removed from the constraints of even the toughest War Powers Act.

In 1971, developments within Allende's Chile and within the Nixon administration set the two on a collision course. In July 1971, the Chilean Congress, although controlled by the opposition Christian Democrat and National parties, unanimously passed a constitutional amendment requiring the Allende administration to nationalize all copper mines. The rich copper reserves of Chile, in just sixty years, had produced for U.S. copper corporations (which included among their largest stockholders the Rockefeller and Morgan financial groups) the equivalent of over half of Chile's total assets accumulated over the previous 400 years. The unanimous vote for the nationalization amendment reflected widespread popular sentiment that the country had been plundered. The amendment called for compensation of the U.S. firms "at book value, less outstanding taxes, depreciation and deductions for obsolescence, depleted lodes and excess profits."

The Congress stipulated that the Comptroller General's Office—somewhat analagous to a mix of the U.S. Supreme Court and the Government Accounting Office—was to determine the "excess profits" by calculating the profits declared during 1955 and 1971 which exceed the 10 percent return considered normal in Chile. The members of the Office of the Comptroller had been appointed before the Allende Administration.[1] They painstakingly weighed the facts of each situation, mine by mine, corporation by corporation. Finally the

Office awarded full book value for two new mines (one owned by Cerro and one owned by Anaconda), but found that in the other mines, the profits of Kennecott and Anaconda already far exceeded (by $774 million) the total book values.

The Chilean declaration that the Chilean copper resources belonged to Chile coincided with a major crisis in the U.S. economy. It was apparent that something had to be done about inflation, unemployment, a negative balance of payments, and massive speculation against the dollar. Although many argued that large U.S. corporations were responsible for the national plight, the crisis atmosphere gave corporate interests the perfect opportunity to assert themselves against any advocates of "moderate" or "flexible" response to foreign "economic nationalism."

The ideological positioning was clear: the U.S. economy was in trouble and it could only be saved by providing total support to U.S. corporations operating abroad. Assistant Treasury Secretary John Petty, a key figure in shaping U.S. policy towards Chile, put it succinctly: "I think you'll find the U.S. less prepared to turn the other cheek. It's a new ball game with new rules." Another high ranking Treasury official reflected the same "hard line": "The time has come when we must assert our own interests—economic as well as political."[2] At the same time, Peter Peterson, former chairman of Bell and Howell and then Assistant to the President for International Economic Policy, issued a major report calling for an activist policy on the part of the U.S. government to protect and expand U.S. business activities abroad. Treasury Secretary Connally echoed the

---

* It should be noted that the capital investment of Kennecott and Anaconda was far less than the book value of the mines. The corporations had also planned to recoup their "losses" through both $121 million worth of U.S. government insurance and tax write-offs of the remaining amount under a questionable Treasury Department authorization to claim the losses as "ordinary" business losses rather than as capital losses—a difference of hundreds of millions of dollars.

government-business partnership, hard-line position in a number of speeches and interviews.[3]

The introduction in August, 1971 of Nixon's New Economic Policy shifted responsibility for the for- mulation of foreign policy towards Latin America from the State Department to the Treasury Department.* Until the N.E.P. and the concommitant Chile "crisis," Latin America seemed to be a low priority in the Nixon Administration. The State Department, under its caretaker, Secretary William Rogers, was generally allowed to administer the "foreign service" in Latin America.[4] In this role the State Department tends to take into account wider political, diplomatic questions and not merely the question of U.S. business profits. In the case of Chile, there are a number of indications that the State Department initially took a "soft line."[5] National Journal reported that Kissinger at first favored a relatively moderate stand toward the Chilean ex- propriations, while Peter Peterson proposed a harder line to discourage other governments from taking similar action.[6]

The decisions and decision-makers of the Treasury Department, on the other hand, are generally more closely linked to U.S. corporation and banking interests than those of the Department of State.* It has come to be considered "natural" that top executives of banks and corporations and their lawyers should do their "civic

---

* It is interesting to note the historical parallel in the Chilean and Cuban situations regarding the formation of U.S. policy. Former Ambassador to Cuba Philip W. Bonsal has written that the Treasury Department, under Secretary Robert Anderson, "called the shots" in defining and implementing the U.S. position toward Cuba prior to the break. Cf. Philip W. Bonsal, *Cuba, Castro and the United States* (Pittsburgh: University of Pittsburgh Press, 1971)

*Kraig Schwartz' "The Socio-Economic Career Patterns of 30 Persons Who Shaped U.S. Policy Toward Latin America" reveals that 70 per cent of the key policy makers during a recent five-year period were from the world of corporate business prior to taking office.

duty" by spending some time as high officials of the Treasury Department. It is no wonder, then, that U.S. interests and policies invariably are defined in terms of the promotion and protection of U.S. corporate holdings.

The Treasury Department under Secretary Connally was certainly no exception to this rule. When Chile dared to try to gain a modicum of freedom from foreign financial domination, it came up against the very same financial giants working out of the Executive branch and dictating U.S. foreign policy. Some of the Key Treasury officials designing the U.S. economic war on Chile were: John M. Hennessey, formerly general manager of the First National City Bank in Lima and La Paz; John R. Petty, formerly a vice president of the Chase Manhattan Bank and now a partner of Lehman Brothers; Paul A. Volcker, formerly an executive of the Chase Manhattan Bank; Charles E. Walker, formerly special assistant to the president of the Republic National Bank of Dallas and former executive vice president and chief lobbyist of the American Bankers Association.

With Treasury Secretary Connally as steward of the New Economic Policy, anything but "moderation" and "flexibility" were the order of the day. Connally, with special access to President Nixon, succeeded in installing the "hard line" against Chile as the policy of the entire Executive Branch. As Professors Pettras and LaPorte conclude, "Once policy had been defined through Connally's initiative, the State Department moved toward the more extreme position, shedding its reservations and "flexibility."[7] By October, 1971, Secretary of State Rogers had taken up the hard business line. In a closed meeting he reassured executives of several U.S. corporations—such as I.T.T., Ford, Anaconda, Ralston Purina, the First National City Bank and the Bank of America—which were threatened by Chilean nationalizations: "The Nixon Administration is a business administration. Its mission is to protect American business." To that end, Rogers made clear, the U.S. would "cut off aid unless she (Chile) provided prompt compensation." When even some of the executives asked Rogers whether this hard line might not be interpreted as a "slap in the face" to Chile and other

Latin American nations, he replied that "such measures might be the only language they understand."[8]

In a characteristically blunt interview, Secretary Connally stated: "The United States can afford to be tough with Latin Americans because we have no friend left there any more. . . ."[9] *Business Week* reported: "Connally is forcing the reopening of debate at top levels on what U.S. policy should be. He is particularly bitter about Latin American hostility toward U.S. investment. . . ."[10] A *New York Times* article concluded that Connally's strategy with Chile was nothing other than a business version of a military domino theory: "Mr. Connally is said to believe that his policy of 'deterrence'—crcking down on Chile—may frighten off other possible expropriating countries."[11] Petras and Laporte in their extensive State Department interviews in late October 1971, found that "the State Department had not been frequently consulted in events since the copper nationalization crisis."[12] In the era of low profile tactics, the Treasury Department has become a central shaper and executor of foreign policy. As one State Department official commented: ". . . Treasury is having an input (into U.S. foreign policy) that it hasn't had in the past."

Following the nationalization of copper in Chile, the National Security Study Memorandum 131 directed that there be an interagency study of current and future policies regarding expropriations. The hard line of the Treasury Department held sway within the Council on International Economic Policy. A major polic statement was drafted and delivered by the Executive on January 19, 1972 with obvious reference to recent expropriations in Chile:

> Thus, when a country expropriates a significant U.S. interest without making reasonable provision for such compensation to U.S. citizens, we will presume that the U.S. will not extend new bilateral economic benefits to the expropriating country. . . . In the face of the expropriatory circumstances just described, we will presume that the United States government will withhold its support from loans under consideration in multilateral development banks.

One of the first actions in the Executive's economic warfare against Chile was implemented through the Treasury Department's Export-Import Bank. Ordinarily countries such as Chile purchase machinery and raw materials from U.S. companies on short- or medium-term credits which are paid back in part out of the sales of products produced by the purchases. These credits—commonly spoken of as the "grease" of international trade—come from the Treasury Department's Export-Import Bank and from loans from private U.S. banks which are guaranteed by the Eximbank. Chile traditionally imported about 40 per cent of its total imports from the U.S. In the 25 years prior to the Allende government, Chile received $600 million worth of direct credits from the Eximbank.

The Eximbank denied the Allende administration's first request for a loan—a request for $21 million to finance part of the purchase of three Boeing passenger jets for the state-owned LAN-Chile airline. In the past, Chile had always received credit for LAN-Chile purchases and had a flawless repayment record. At the time of the request (early 1971), U.S. officials admitted that Chile had been scrupulous in paying its debts, a fact confirmed by a Commerce Department official's admission that Chile's "credit worthiness" was not the real problem.[13] Obviously, the decision to deny the request was political.

In August, Eximbank president, Henry Kearns, informed Chile's ambassador in Washington that Chile could expect no loans or guarantees until the question of compensation for U.S. mining and other interests in Chile had been resolved. According to a *New York Times* article (August 1, 1971), the State Department indicated that the decision to block Eximbank loans to Chile was "made on the White House level," under pressure from American companies.

The Eximbank not only made it impossible for Chile to get new credits for urgently needed purchases in the U.S., but also cut off the disbursements of the direct loans previously negotiated. In addition, the Eximbank suspended the guarantee and insurance program for commercial banks and exporters (through the Eximbank affiliate, the Foreign Credit Insurance Association—the FCIA). Private banks and suppliers immediately took the cue from the Treasury's Eximbank. This short term credit cut-off was tantamount to the formal blockade of Cuba—only it was "low profile" and thus did not run the risk of attack by Congress or public opinion.

The total impact on Chile was devastating. By 1972, not only had Chile's imports declined but the percentage of total imports from the U.S. plummeted from 40 per cent to around 15 per cent.[14] The lack of replacement parts for machinery of U.S. origin (the bulk of machinery in Chile) brought about serious production bottlenecks. The forced decline in imports mainly affected the middle class which was accustomed to imported goods and services. (The large lower class actually experienced improved access to basic goods[15] and the upper class developed a thriving black market which President Allende was powerless to close down since the opposition parties which controlled the Congress basically supported the gameplan of provoking economic chaos.) The impact was most serious in the Chilean transportation sector since a large percentage of all buses and trucks are GM or Ford models. Already by early 1972, 30 per cent of the privately owned "microbuses," 21 per cent of the taxibuses and 33 per cent of the state-owned buses were immobilized because of the lack of parts.[16]Owners of the private trucks, whose strike in large measure sparked the crisis which provided the pretext for the coup, often cited their inability to obtain replacements for their trucks as a reason for their strike.

"Multilateral" Institutions

The Nixon Administration used its clout within the so-called multilateral institutions, such as the Inter-American Development Bank (the I.D.B.) and the World Bank, to reenforce policies calculated to strangle the Chilean economy. The Allende government continued to pay off old loans to the banks, yet neither institution made new loans to Chile.

In the I.D.B. the U.S. Executive's appointees wield veto power over loans. (The U.S. has 40 per cent of the votes and a two-thirds vote is required to approve a loan.) From 1959 to the election of the Allende government, the I.D.B. granted an exceptional number of loans to Chile—59 loans totalling over $310 million. In 1971 the Allende government requested several new loans, some of which were considered for preliminary examination by an I.D.B. special mission which visited Chile in June 1971. At that time, the bank's representatives and the Chilean authorities agreed to promote a petrochemical complex—a perfect "development" project, transferring technology and capable of earning foreign exchange. The loan was never granted, however, and other well-researched and reasonable requests for electric power and natural (liquid) gas were never fulfilled. The Bank even denied emergency relief for the victims of the 1971 earthquake. Chile, nevertheless, continued to pay off its debt to the I.D.B. In 1971 and 1972, Chile paid back around $16 million. With no new loans granted, Chile ironically found itself a net capital exporter to the Inter-American Development Bank.

The usual excuse for not making any new loans to Chile was that Chile was "economically unstable," not "credit worthy," and in an unfavorable exchange position. While Chile's exchange position was greatly weakened by the plummeting price of copper on the world market and the oligarchs' flight of capital, just as great a factor was the U.S. credit blockade. Supposedly, the very purpose of the I.D.B. is to help Latin American nations overcome economic problems. But, as a member of the I.D.B. staff put it, "The I.D.B. is behaving like an umbrella that's up only when it's not raining." Severe economic problems in Chile hardly began with the election of Allende. The I.D.B. poured millions into Chile during previous economic crises. The only discernable difference was that while the policies of previous administrations may not have solved economic problems in Chile, they were favorable to the interests of Washington and Wall Street.

Chile's economic problems did not impede the I.D.B. from making two revealing exceptions to its "boycott" of Chile. It granted a $7 million loan to the Catholic University and $4.6 million to the Austral University (in Chile's conservative, dominantly German-speaking region), both increasingly strongholds of anti-U.P. activities and centers of purges of the U.P. sympathizers.

The policy of the World Bank was similar. The U.S. Governor of the Bank is under the Treasury Secretary.* Prior to the election of Allende, the Bank had lent Chile $234,650,000. After the election of Allende, Robert McNamara's Bank refused all loan requests without exception. The Bank refused requests for, among others, a fruit-growing project; the second stage of a cattle breeding program (the first stage was begun under Frei with World Bank assistance); and an ongoing electrification program (which for the twenty previous years had been actively supported by the Bank).

It is revealing to consider the Bank's purported reason for turning down the electrification project. The Bank demanded that the Chilean government raise electricity rates; the Allende government had adopted a rate schedule favorable to the poor, small consumer. The Popular Unity government refused to change basic worker-oriented policies just to try to please the World Bank, and the loan was refused.

Mr. McNamara, over the past three years, has eloquently deplored the economic policies of such countries as Brazil which promote even greater income and wealth concentration. Yet the Bank continued to make massive, record loans to Brazil, while cutting off all assistance to a Chilean government struggling to achieve the development goals McNamara claimed to advocate. Not satisfied with cutting off loans, Mr. McNamara, in a sharp departure from normal multilateral diplomacy, spoke out with special aggressiveness against the Allende government and in such a way as to damage Chile's world credit rating.

In contrast with the I.D.B. and the World Bank, Chile

---

* The control of the U.S. Executive in the I.D.B. and the World Bank is not always overt since the U.S. has never formally voted against a loan request, partly because the bank boards operate by consensus and thus issues on which there is disagreement are not brought to formal vote.

has had no problems with the International Monetary Fund (I.M.F.). In 1971 and 1972, the Allende government received $148 million from the I.M.F. in partial compensation for the fallen copper price and from its normal allotment of drawing rights. Such a "business-as-usual" attitude on the part of the I.M.F. again raises questions about the real criteria for the I.D.B. and World Bank cutoff. I.M.F. policies towards Chile might well be attributed to the strong European influence in the I.M.F. and the consequently weaker U.S. influence. When last year the United States tried to oust president Pierre-Paul Schweitzer, Chile rallied Latin American members to his support.

Footnotes

1. cf. Interview with the president of Cerro Corporation, C. Gordon Murphy: "The tribunal is completely independent of the President, I can assure you." *Business Week,* December 9, 1972.

2. Mark L. Chadwin, "Foreign Policy Report: Nixon Administration Debates New Position Paper on Latin America," *National Journal,* Part I, January 15, 1972, p. 97.

3. See, for instance, Frank K. Fowlkes, "Economic Report/Connally revitalizes Treasury, Assumes Stewardship of Nixon's New Economic Policy." *National Journal,* Vol. II, October 2, 1971, p. 1991.

4. This low priority was confirmed in interviews with State Department officials by James Petras and Robert LaPorte, Jr., "Chile: No," *Foreign Policy,* Summer, 1972.

5. Chadwin, Part II, p. 152; Petras and LaPorte, passim.

6. Dom Bonafede, "Peterson Unit Helps Shape Tough International Economic Policy," *National Journal,* Vol. III, November 13, 1971, p. 2245.

7. Petras and LaPorte, op. cit.

8. cf. Benjamin Welles, *The New York Times,* October 23, 1971.

9. *New York Times,* August 15, 1971.

10. *Business Week,* July 10, 1971.

11. *New York Times,* August 15, 1971.

12. Petras and LaPorte, op. cit.

13. *Wall Street Journal,* June 4, 1971.

14. World Bank, I.D.A. and I.F.C., "Policies and Operations," Washington, June, 1969, p. 3.

15. cf. survey in the opposition-controlled weekly, *Ercilla,* September, 1972.

16. *Chile Hoy,* August 11-17, 1972.

Chile's Foreign Debt

The analysis presented below was compiled somewhat before the military coup by a group of U.S. Christians stationed in Chile belonging to the "Project for Awareness and Action" (PARA).

The following is a report on the present state of the talks regarding the renegotiations of Chile's debt to the United States. Negotiating teams from both countries met in December of 1972 and again in March of this year. At present it appears that the talks have reached an impasse. Chile is seeking to renegotiate the terms of the debt; a normal procedure between loaning and recipient nations when the recipient nation is unable to meet its payments on schedule. The United States is assuming a hard line in regard to Chile's request. The basic issue at stake between the two nations, along with a possible solution that would avoid a confrontation at the present time, is the subject of this paper.

The United States position at the two rounds of talks appears to have been the following: Chile has put a "big rock" in the path of Chile-United States relations. The big rock is the deductions made because of the concept of excess profits which resulted in the nationalization of the American copper companies without indemnification. The United States backs up the claims of the copper companies for an adequate cash settlement, and therefore must spread a few "pebbles" in Chile's path. Some of these pebbles would be refusal to renegotiate the Chilean debt, votation against Chilean credit requests in the international lending organizations, elimination of credit for purchase of American products, etc. However, if the Chileans were willing to remove the "rock," there would be no problem in removing the "pebbles."

Chile's position is that the concept of excessive profits is just, considering the injustice of present international economic structures, and the fact that it is explicitly called for in Chile's constitution. Chile cites the United Nations Charter which legalizes nationalizations which are carried out constitutionally. Shortly after the 1970 presidential elections in Chile the Chilean Congress, including the center-right Christian Democrat Party and the rightist National Party, approved a constitutional reform which authorized the nationalization of foreign-owned companies engaged in the exploitation of natural resources. One of the key articles of this reform authorized that excessive profits signed by foreign investors (more than a 12 percent annual profit) could be deducted from the actual value of the nationalized property. In this manner, when the value of the excessive profits was deducted from the price set for Anaconda and Kennecott mining interest, no cash payment was found to be necessary.

This concept of excessive profits has been the main impasse between the United States and Chile ever since, and it could even be the cause of a rupture in diplomatic relations between the two countries. Such a rupture would not be in the best interests of either the American or the Chilean people. For Chile this is a point that cannot be compromised. And from the point of the many under-developed nations whose natural resources are being exploited by foreign interests, it is a principle which should not be compromised.

There does not appear to exist at least one alternative to an immediate conflict between Chile and the United States. Ever since 1916 there has existed a treaty between two nations for the express purpose of providing solutions to difficult questions which cannot be resolved through normal diplomatic channels. The treaty establishes a permanent five-member international commission whose purpose is to study disagreements between the two countries and to report on possible solutions in order to avoid direct conflict. The commission is formed by two members designated by each country, only one of which may be from that country, and a fifth member who heads the commission and who is designated by common agreement. At the present moment Chile has designated its two members. They are the Polish international law expert Manfred Lachs who presently is a member of the International Court of the Hague, and Edmundo Vargas, professor of international law at the University of Chile. The fifth member has also been designated by common agreement (during the administration of John F. Kennedy). She is Madam Suzan Bastid, a respected professor of international law at the University of Paris. The American designations are now vacant since both have died without being re-placed.

Article Three of the treaty requires that when a question between the two countries cannot be resolved through normal bilateral diplomatic procedures it must immediately be referred to the permanent commission. The commission will study the question and provide a full report within one year. Each country will then have six months to study the conclusions reached by the commission, and then try to reach a mutual agreement. If this proves impossible the question can then be sent to the International Court of the Hague, except when the question involves national security or other grave aspects.

During the negotiations in March of this year Chile proposed that, due to the impasse, it was willing to allow its interpretation of the nationalization proceedings be studied by the international commission according to the treaty. The United States negotiators recognized that the treaty was effective and obligatory in this instance, but they gave a very firm but informal "no." They also let it be known that the position of the United States in the upcoming Paris talks for the renegotiation of Chile's international debts would be even more stringent than it has been to date. The most recent development in the case occurred on May 24th when U.S. Secretary of State William Rogers spoke with Chilean President Salvador Allende during the inauguration of the new president of Argentina in Buenos Aires. Rogers informed Allende that the United States government would announce its formal position concerning the acceptance or rejection of the use of the treaty within three weeks.\ Ed. note: This announcement was never made.]

The renegotiation of the debt and the nationalization of the copper companies are two separate and distinct issues. The U.S. attempt to unite the two issues during these negotiations is a clear example of government protection of private investment in foreign countries. A continuing "hard line" on the part of the U.S. in this matter could lead to a rupturing of Chile-U.S. relations. Such a rupture would be to the interests of neither country.

New York Times, November 12, 1973: Private U.S. Loan in Chile Up Sharply

JONATHAN KANDELL

There has been a dramatic turnaround in the availability of private United States bank loans for Chile in the wake of the overthrow of the Marxist coalition government by a military coup last September.

On Friday, for example, the Manufacturers Hanover Trust Company announced here it was extending to a Chilean bank a $24 million loan. Reliable banking sources asserted that Manufacturers Hanover had extended an additional $20 million to this country's Central Bank. The announced loan is the largest credit extended to Chile by an American bank since before the late Marxist President Salvador Allende assumed office three years ago.

According to financial sources here, eight to ten American and two Canadian banks have offered Chile commercial loans totalling about $150 million since the military junta took office.

All the financing—including those by Manufacturers Hanover—are short-term commercial credits requiring repayment within an 18-month to three-year period.

Short-term credits generally are not used to finance development or new investments, but rather to meet immediate obligations, such as import bills and payments on outstanding business debts.

Under the government of President Jorge Alessandri, a Conservative, from 1958 to 1964, and Eduardo Frei, a center-leftist, from 1964 to 1970, Chile normally had available about $300 million in short-term commercial credits, mainly from American banks.

Credits Dry Up

But almost as soon as President Allende's government assumed office in November, 1970, such credits dried up. By the middle of this year, short-term commercial loans to Chile from American banks had dropped to about $30 million.

These loans are usually an indication of the faith that commercial banks have in a country's ability to repay. Business sources here noted that a lack of confidence in the Allende government based largely on ideological reasons was further aggravated by the late President's declaration of a moratorium on the repayment of most debts in November, 1971.

Throughout his term in office, President Allende repeatedly charged that the United States government was discouraging American commercial banks and other international financial sources from extending credits to his country.

American Intervention

A final blow came when Chile nationalized, without compensation, the holding of three large United States-based copper companies—Kennecott, Anaconda and the Cerro Corporation. After that most American aid was confined to miitary and humanitarian areas.

The American government intervened to prevent Chile from receiving credit from the Export-Import Bank for airplanes and loans from the Inter American Development Bank and the World Bank to promote petrochemical and agricultural development.

The virulently anti-Marxist military junta moved quickly to try to regain the confidence of American banks and investors.

For one thing, it almost immediately declared that it would honor Chile's foreign debts, which had mushroomed to almost $3.5 billion under the economic chaos which developed during the Allende regime.

The junta has also announced its intention to return to private hands "the vast majority" of the more than 300 foreign and domestic concerns that were taken over by the Allende government without compensation. Among these are about 40 which have American investment.

And perhaps most important, as far as the American government and private companies are concerned, the junta has announced that it is prepared to resume negotiations on compensation to the United States copper companies. Their assets in Chile have been variously estimated at $500 to $700 million. President Allende refused to pay compensation on the grounds that the concerns owed Chile $774 million in what he called excess profits.

Another, less tangible, reason for the restoration of American business confidence in Chile is the fact that many of the "old faces" that left key financial institutions after Dr. Allende assumed office have now returned.
Under the Marxist government, virtually all banks fell under de facto control. Although the opposition-controlled Congress refused to approve legislation nationalizing banks, the government took over these institutions through the purchase of majority shares, seizures without compensation, or by requisition.

Although the military junta has not indicated what it will do about control of the banks, it has returned former managers to the help of many of the private ones taken over by the Allende government.

For example, the head of the Banco de Chile—the most important private bank here and the recipient of the $24 million loan from Manufacturer's Hanover—is once again Manuel Vinagre, who headed the bank before Dr. Allende assumed office. He is well known and trusted by American bankers.

Grain Credit Awarded to the Junta

The following statement was released by the U.S. Department of Agriculture regarding the financing by the Commodity Credit Corporation (CCC) of a $24 million wheat purchase made by the new government on September 26, 1973.

The Department's export market service this morning established a line of CCC credit for the export of U.S. wheat to Chile. The line was for $24 million or about 120,000 tons with repayment over 3 years in 3 equal annual installments of principal and accrued interest. The current interest rate for CCC credit is 9½ per cent or 10½ per cent per annum depending whether an American or foreign bank is used for the guarantor.

The credit line is expected to help reestablish the long term market relationship which U.S. wheat has had in Chile as well as to ease the current food situation there. Several years ago the U.S. was exporting 120,000 to 140,000 tons of wheat annually to Chile. Exports declined to negligible amounts during the past two years.

A DEBATE ON THE CHILEAN COUP

The November 2, 1973 editorial page of the Wall Street Journal *contained some of the most controversial material which had appeared on the makings of the coup and what it had left in its wake. The various points raised in that issue of the* Journal *are challenged in the following article by* IDOC's *editor which appeared in the December 3, 1973 edition of the* Nation. *Efforts were made to secure the rights to reprint the original articles which had been published in the* Journal, *but that publication declined granting them. Following the* Nation *article is an exchange of letters between Everett G. Martin, the* Journal's *Latin America correspondent, and Laurence R. Birns, which appeared in the January 19, 1974 issue of the* Nation; *it should be noted that the Birns response was originally 12 manuscript pages in length, but was necessarily abridged for reasons of space by the* Nation's *editors.*

The Nation, December 3, 1973: Chile in the *Wall Street Journal*

LAURENCE R. BIRNS

On November 2, *The Wall Street Journal* devoted some two-thirds of its editorial page to the military overthrow of the constitutional government of Chile, its causes and its aftermath. It chose three lines of inquiry to develop its principal theses: the extent of the violence visited upon the nation; the quantity of public support that the Allende government had behind it immediately before its demise, and the achievements, on balance, of President Allende's tenure. Taken together, the three separate contributions which appeared on that page make up one of the most provocative ventures in American journalism of recent times.

One of the articles was "Those Horror Tales from Chile," by Pablo Huneeus. Several weeks earlier, Everett Martin, the *Journal's* Latin American correspondent, had referred to Huneeus as "one of Chile's leading sociologists." At the time, I found this description puzzling since I had known several members of Huneeus' family but had heard hardly any reference to him in Chilean intellectual circles. I have tried, therefore, to check closely into Huneeus' professional status, which I thought it important to establish, since the major thrust of his article is the contention that John Barnes, foreign correspondent of *Newsweek*, was inaccurate in his estimate of the number of bodies he had seen in the

Santiago morgue ("Slaughterhouse in Santiago," *Newsweek,* October 8). Without question the Barnes piece was the most influential one on the Chilean coup to appear in the American press; it was a major factor in moving Senator Kennedy and the U.S. Senate to pass an amendment to the foreign aid bill which would restrict to humanitarian purposes U.S. assistance to Chile.

It has been established that Huneeus is a well-spoken, widely traveled and charming man who can hardly be called a leader of Chile's sociological community. He is himself of aristocratic background and has made two socially brilliant marriages.His first wife, Delia Vegara, is one of Chile's two female graduates of Columbia's School of Journalism and editor of *Paula,* the nation's foremost women's magazine. It was for this magazine, I've been told, that Huneeus had done some of his professional writing. *Paula* can be thought of as a more discreet cross between *Vogue* and *Cosmopolitan,* and Huneeus was something of its Joyce Brothers.

For part of the Allende period, he was out of the country on an extended honeymoon in the Spanish Mediterranean after his second marriage. Huneeus is part of the Zapallar set, frequenting Chile's upper classes. A member of the right wing of the Christian Democratic Party (PDC), he some time ago addressed a party meeting on the Allende administration's vulgarity and lack of culture. After watching him on television, one member of his own PDC faction described Huneeus' beliefs as being barely distinguishable from those of the rank and file in Patria y Libertad, the nation's most extreme right-wing movement.

The Wall Street Journal editors vouch for him as "a Chilean known to us as being objective and independent," an endorsement that would seem to strain the meaning of those adjectives. Huneeus emerges, rather, as a man who by breeding and experience would find Populist or Socialist politics anathema, and the *Journal's* decision to use him as one of its windows into Chile casts reasonable doubt on its own objectivity. On September 20, Everett Martin introduced Huneeus to *Journal* readers as an intellectual whom he had sought out as part of his endeavor to supply a broad view of Chilean realities. By November 2, the association is closer: the editors identify Huneeus as a "journalist and professor of sociology at the University of Chile, who previously has assisted American correspondents, including those of *The Wall Street Journal* and *Newsweek*, in preparation of reports on Chile."

Presumably he did not assist John Barnes on his story of October 8. Huneeus is utterly skeptical of Barnes's account of his four visits to the Santiago morgue, raising even the possibility that he was never there at all. The accuracy of the *Newsweek* correspondent's body count at the morgue is important, because the military junta that overthrew the Allende government on September 11 and now rules Chile has attempted to minimize the ensuing casualties and thus the magnitude of the violence to which the nation has been subjected. It has consistently issued unrealistically low figures—as late as September 16, the junta was maintaining that only ninety-five people had been killed in the fighting. At about the same time, the CIA intelligence estimates were that some 2,000 to 3,000 people had been killed, and those were the minimum figures that the bulk of the European press was using; some reputable correspondents were claiming that scores of thousands had fallen. For the junta, therefore, it was of pressing importance that the John Barnes article be discredited: it was playing havoc with the new regime's public relations abroad, particularly in the United States.

It is to this task that Pablo Huneeus vigorously directs himself. He questioned the morgue's resident doctors and staff as to the accuracy of the Barnes article. He was told that Barnes was lying when he said that he had seen fifty bodies strewn in a corridor. And as to the 2,796 bodies which Barnes says the daughter of a staff member told him had been processed through the morgue since the coup, the reactions are "what brilliant imagination"—"what an exaggeration!"

But supposing that Huneeus has reported accurately what he was told, what is the value of that evidence? He does not tell his readers that the Medical College of Chile (the equivalent of the American Medical Association) is an extremely conservative organization; that it was a mainstay of the massive anti-government middle-class strikes of October 1972 and immediately preceding Allende's overthrow; that it had stubbornly opposed the establishment of clinics in the poorer districts, insisting that medical services must be dispensed from hospitals (which are often many miles from the slums that ring Santiago), and that since the overthrow it had militantly supported the junta.

Political bias aside, is it reasonable to suppose that anyone working as a public servant today in Chile would dispute official junta statements? In the days immediately preceding Huneeus' trip to the morgue, books were being burned in the streets, machine guns were being held at the heads of children during nocturnal raids on private homes (including those of an American network correspondent and of the former rector of Santiago's Catholic University), people who disappeared from working-class districts were later reported killed while "attempting to escape." Barnes himself admits that he got into the morgue only because those on duty there were careless; it was scarcely to their advantage to substantiate his story. But Huneeus does not take such factors into account; as "one of Chile's leading sociologists," he strolls over to the morgue and has a chat with the people he finds there, as though Santiago were as relaxed a city as Geneva.

Friends in the European section of the U.N. Secretariat have given me a copy of a cable sent from Santiago to UNESCO, Paris, on October 5. It is signed by Luis Ramallo, at that time acting secretary-general of the U.N.-affiliated Latin American Faculty of Social Science (FLACSO). Among other matters, the cable refers to the abduction and subsequent violent death of a young Bolivian, Jorge Rios, who was a student at FLACSO. While Mr. Ramallo was recently in New York, I showed him my copy of the cable and he verified it. I also asked him about his observations at the morgue, which he visited on September 19 in search of Rios. Ramallo said that the room in which he had counted approximately 185 bodies was apparently not the one where Barnes saw the bodies that he described, but he confirmed Barnes's description of the entrance to the morgue and the physical surroundings of the anteroom through which Barnes had passed.

After talking with Ramallo, I got in touch with *Newsweek*, and several hours later he and Barnes met me in my office where, using a makeshift diagram of the morgue's layout, they confirmed each other's account of the building and of what they both had seen. This encounter between Barnes and Ramallo became part of *Newsweek's* response to the *Journal's* attack on its accuracy, which appeared in the latter's issue of November 15.

When Ramallo made his morgue visit, he went first through the front door to get a pass, and then went out and re-entered the building through the ambulance entrance; he was accompanied by a Protestant minister. Passing along a hallway containing a number of coffins, he was shown into a large room to look for the body of Rios. Huneeus had quoted a Dr. Vargas, "an elderly experienced doctor," as dismissing Barnes's tally of the bodies he had seen, on the ground that he was suffering from "perception shock." To illustrate the effect of this reaction, Vargas said: "When there are ten bodies together many persons can't even recognize their wives or fathers." That, said the doctor, is what "must have happened to that correspondent, presuming he ever got into the morgue."

For Luis Ramallo, Huneeus and Dr. Vargas will have to provide another explanation, because he and his associate spent more than an hour in one of the morgue's rooms. And shortly thereafter he said in his cable that he had found his student's "bullet ridden body with signs of multiple concussions and two large gaping wounds in chest and legs. Body was found among some 150 [he chose a figure lower than his actual count] similarly unidentified and wounded bodies in the public mortuary where it had been deposited by military.

Discounting the five children (three little boys and two little girls), one of whom, in death, was gripping his father's leg, and the small number of women, Ramallo had to peer into the face of almost every naked cadaver in the room, looking for his student. He noticed that the bulk of them appeared to be of working-class origin, that a number of them had mangled limbs, and that the majority of them had been shot. He guessed that they were all recently dead because attendants were mopping up blood after several bodies had been moved, and there was no smell in the room, even though it was not air-conditioned. He did not find Rios' body in that room and an attendant then told him it might be in an adjoining room. On entering, Ramallo realized that he was in the morgue proper, for he could feel cooling and noticed the sliding shelves common to such places. In this room, he found Rios' body. One of the things which Ramallo recalls from this visit was an offhand comment by one of the doctors that they no longer had time to make individual autopsies, and that many corpses received only visual certification of the causes of death.

Huneeus makes the point that the list of the cadavers on the door of the mortuary was consecutively numbered. He then says that the figure of 2,796 bodies cited by Barnes was actually the total for all of 1973. Mr. Ramallo saw a list of some 130 names posted on the door when he paid his visit, and of this number, two-thirds had the word "unidentified" next to them. He reports also the interesting fact that, under the column giving the source of the bodies, the bulk of the notations cited such authorities as the "Tacna Regiment," "naval patrol," etc. There is enough evidence in Mr. Ramallo's narrative to establish that during the period immediately after the uprising the morgue was being inundated with the victims of violent deaths, that the morgue itself was under military control, that there was no reason to believe that anyone would readily tell the truth, that the occasion when Mr. Huneeus visited the morgue was perhaps many days after Barnes had been there and that, whatever the accuracy of the statement made by the daughter of an official to *Newsweek's* correspondent, things were far from normal at the morgue, or for that matter in Santiago.

Given Mr. Huneeus' background, his complaint about

the "journalistic imperialism" of *Newsweek* and his statement that this "rich American magazine sends from London a British correspondent a week after the coup" (Barnes has long journalistic experience in Latin America) because "he only wants to use us for a story that will sell" must be taken with a wry smile. It is a wonder that, with the dismembered ruin of his nation lying around him, a large number of his fellow journalists and academics in jail or dead; with many of the nation's newspaper and radio stations closed down (the remainder being censored); the universities purged; and the military acting as the Praetorian overseers of national institutions, Huneeus can say with an almost palpable shrug that "it's sad so many died, but it's good so many survived."

While Huneeus does add, "Not that I am happy with the junta," he mentions not one thing that causes him unhappiness. And his remark that "Every Chilean feels that, no matter how low the death toll, what happened is a tragedy," is patently untrue. The post-overthrow celebrations that occurred in middle-class neighborhoods suggest that a large number of political opportunists and those whose economic interests had suffered are perfectly content with the way things have turned out. At best, they deplore the death toll. And to offset the killings and the oustings, there is now more room in the university faculties, hospitals, media and professional life for those who were, or thought themselves, slighted during the Allende years. (Unlike those now out of favor, they were able to voice their opposition to the government and their lives and those of their families were secure.)

For the *Journal's* editors, Allende got what he deserved— "The generals took care of him before he and his assassination crews could get to them." This apparently refers to "Plan Z," a document as well authenticated as the Protocols of the Elders of Zion. This alleged plot was trotted out several days after the coup, when a justification was needed quickly to placate the world outcry over the carnage. The *Journal* editorializes on November 2: "it is amazing there's been as little bloodshed as there has." Apparently, the minimum CIA figure (a more accurate figure might be from 7,000 to 10,000) is trivial.

Or does the *Journal* base its estimates on the reporting of Everett Martin, who has been their Latin American correspondent for several years, having previously been *Newsweek's* correspondent in Vietnam? Martin is a decent, well-meaning man, who has been far more ready than most U.S. correspondents to go out in the field for a story. The questions to be asked are what preconceptions does he take with him and how does he go about acquiring his information? Unfortunately, he is often unreliable as to facts and, although he is diligent, his insights are open to question. Since Martin began reporting on Chile, I have compiled a list of eighty-five of his most obvious mistakes of fact and interpretation.

Characteristic of such lapses were Mr. Martin's efforts in the piece he contributed to the *Journal's* November 2nd issue, entitled ". . . a Few Loud Echoes from Academia." Martin is troubled that ". . . so many misleading reports and analyses of the events surrounding the coup in Chile . . . have appeared in reputable" segments of the media. While slightly separating himself from Huneeus when he says that ". . . there have been killings and executions that certainly seem excessive," Martin is still convinced of *Newsweek's* misrepresentation of the facts" and is distressed by the "presentation of much more insidious and subtle articles"—namely E. Bradford Burns's observations on the Chile coup which appeared in *The Nation* of October 29. Martin is specifically unhappy with Professor Burns's tally of a pro-Allende parade, but he is generally unhappy with the activities of the academics, for there isn't ". . . much that's accurate or useful in the colored accounts the U.S. academic community is currently putting out on the subject."

Since I'm a member of that community and since I'm on record as having said in the *New York Review of Books* (November 1) that Mr. Martin's reportage on Chile is helping to "construct a mythology designed to show that Allende was responsible for his own fall," I feel personally involved. In another publication, I hope to evaluate some of the economic statistics he has been providing since he began writing on Chile. I can say provisionally that only occasionally do they conform to generally accepted data.

In the *Nation* article which Martin attacks, Burns puts the number of people who participated in the pro-Allende parade of September 4 at more than 800,000. Martin insists that at most there were 20,000. Both Martin and I know that, in the fervent atmosphere of Chilean politics, it has long been easy for both the government and the opposition to muster massive parades at short notice. Foreign observers have often marveled at this ability. In an article dated July 6, Martin himself noted that ". . . so far Chile's economic problems haven't apparently eroded President Allende's base of popular support." Yet a scant two months later, he is intent on establishing that it was difficult for the government to mobilize a large outpouring of supporters, and had to resort to tricks to bolster the crowd's apparent size. Says Martin, the Allendistas chose the Plaza de la Constitucion for their demonstration because its comparatively confined quarters would make it seem that more people were present. He and several colleagues (unnamed) ". . . noted that a large contingent marched around and around one block to make it look larger."

The facts are as follows: the plan was to have all the paraders (not just the group Martin mentions) march around the reviewing stands, which were in the Plaza. For six hours, four columns of marchers converged on the Plaza and then passed back to the Alameda, the city's principal thoroughfare and three or four times as wide as New York's Fifth Avenue. The crowd filled the Alameda from the Plaza Italia to the vicinity of the Moneda, the Presidential palace, a distance of at least ten city blocks. Conservatively put by the opposition, the crowd numbered 300,000. Others used figures closer to a million. Whatever Professor Burns's abilities as a crowd counter, they are superior to those of Mr. Martin.

Actually, it is possible that Martin got his demonstrations mixed up. In another article he says that ". . . at least 300,000 women gathered in Santiago to demand that President Allende resign." That demonstration, which occurred on September 5, extended the short distance between Catholic University and the UNCTAD building and, given the limitations of space, it couldn't possibly have numbered more than 15,000 to 30,000 people.

In his November 2nd article, Martin writes of ". . . mounting evidence that there was considerable fraud during the Congressional election for the government to achieve the 44 per cent total" of the vote which it won. This "mounting evidence" was actually the fabrication of one man, Jaime del Valle, dean of the Law School of Catholic University. Soon after he made this charge, he appeared on one of Chile's most popular television talk shows (having previously asked its director not to press him on the "fraud" issue), and in the presence of the director of the nation's electoral college, himself a member of the opposition Christian Democrats, was forced to reveal that he had no evidence. It should also be noted that the opposition-controlled Congress did not support the allegation of any sizable electoral fraud. Somewhat later, del Valle was overheard admitting to the rector of his university that he had invented the charge in order to provide the opposition with a little ammunition against the government.

Almost alone of foreign correspondents, Martin believes that "the armed forces were loyal to the government and were the last to turn against him." In that case, one might ask, who were the first? Jonathan Kandell of *The New York Times* wrote a long article on the plotting of the coup a number of weeks ago. His conclusion was that the military had begun to conspire almost a year earlier and that it soon reached the point of being determined to go through with the deed, whatever the circumstances. Rather than accept the official account, Mr. Martin might seek out interviews with Gen. Manuel Torres de la Cruz, Adm. Jose Toribio Merino, a Valparaiso right-wing priest by the name of Osvaldo Lira, and read back issues of a publication called *Tizona*. He might also explore the role of Jaime Guzman, now the junta's leading ideological mentor, and the ultra-montane "Movement for the Protection of the Family, Tradition, and Property." That group had close ties with similar groups in Brazil and elsewhere in Latin America, and was particularly active in proselytizing the navy (at its Valparaiso headquarters) against the government.

Furthermore, Martin's statement that the military's loyalty to the Allende government is evidenced by its having joined his Cabinet on three separate occasions somewhat obscures what actually happened. It wasn't as Mr. Martin suggests, so much that Allende wanted the military to join him as that the opposition parties insisted that it do so as a precondition for settling economic and other difficulties. Nor does the record agree with Martin's contention that, far from advocating Chile's continuing to receive American military assistance, ". . . it was Dr. Allende's opponents who resent the U.S. aid to the Chilean military. . . ." One would like to see one official or nonofficial statement from either of the two major opposition parties that would uphold this allegation.

And Martin seems to have recurring trouble with figures. In an article published a day after the coup, he gives the size of the Chilean army as 25,000 men; the navy, 5,000; and the air force, 5,000. In the 1973-74 listing by the prestigious London-based Institute of Strategic Studies, the figures are respectively, 32,000, 18,000 and 10,000. Martin also has trouble with chronology. Several paragraphs later in the same piece, he writes: "Last January, while the three chiefs of staff were still in the cabinet, Mr. Allende was pressured to allow passage of a bill. It gave the military the right to search for and to seize all illegal arms in the country." But that bill was passed the previous year and had gone unimplemented for many months. It can be persuasively argued that the military search squads began energetically to carry out raids (mainly against left-wing arms caches) only when plans for the military coup had matured and the need to strip potential adversaries was at hand.

Another issue raised by Martin is that "the professors want to forget" that back in April 1971, when the pro-Allende forces mustered 50 per cent in the municipal elections (in the September 1970 elections their tally had been 36.2 per cent), they pointed out that Allende was no longer a minority President. But after the March 1973 Congressional elections, when the government coalition received only 44 per cent of the vote, they conveniently forgot the slide from the earlier vote of 50 per cent. But if Martin were conversant with modern Chilean history, he would know that almost invariably the Chilean electorate votes in larger numbers for the seated President in the first election after he has taken office than it has originally, and that also it invariably votes against him in the midterm one. Allende's popular predecessor, President Frei, a Christian Democrat, experienced a similar precipitous rise and decline of support. The important feature of the March Congressional election was that, despite the dislocations, the food shortages and the dismal short-term economic prospects for the nation, the electorate voted in significantly larger numbers for the government candidates than it had in 1970. Considering the patterns of Chilean history, that was an exceedingly important achievement.

Martin speaks of corruption within the overthrown government. Of course there was corruption. But, given the difficult circumstances of the nation, and the basic middle-class background of most of the leftist administrators and managers, would Martin and the *Journal* maintain that corruption was at a level to justify the destruction of much of the civic decency that formerly characterized the Chilean nation? There were no political prisoners under Allende, and under his rule, the broad range of all the freedoms was maintained. Compare what existed then with what exists today. On a deeper level, there is implicit the inference that democratic procedures are only for good times and when a business-oriented regime is in power. When a regime committed to social justice and a redistribution of national wealth comes into office, different ground rules are apparently in effect. The *Journal* and Martin speak repeatedly of Allende's minority government, but in fact, except for the Frei years, every Chilean president in the 20th century has won office only with a plurality. And the fact that the opposition did win a majority vote during Allende's tenure does not justify Martin's conclusion that a majority of the public advocated the violent, bloody overthrow of the constitutional government.

The *Journal's* staff could have approached the Chilean economy from a different direction. Martin dismisses those U.S. academicians who attribute Chile's economic difficulties to the fact ". . . that Chile has always had economic problems and anyhow all the difficulties were caused by the U.S. credit blockade." But is he prepared to deny that Chile had one of the most archaic and stagnant oligarchy-controlled economies in all of Latin America, or that Allende inherited one of the highest per capita national debts in the world? Granted that Allende's economic policies would win him no friends in the American business community, isn't it true that the cutoff of supplier credits from the United States and the aborting of development loans from the regional and international agencies, together with a falling market for copper through much of the Allende years, would have placed an insuperable burden on the best-managed of economies?

Martin goes on to say that in fact the Allende regime "received more international credit than any other Chilean government in history." He cites no figures, but even if his statement is accurate, what does it mean? For the most part, Allende's Chile received only bilateral credits, spaced over a period of years. (Supplier credits from the United States all but disappeared.) For any one year, the figure probably fell significantly under the inflation-adjusted credit flows which occurred during the Frei era. In any event, these credits were for specific goods from specific countries. They did not permit Chile to buy on the open market and were of little use in buying the replacement parts and components needed for industrial and transportation systems geared to equipment manufactured in the United States.

While I would certainly not blame all of the Allende administration's economic problems on the United States' systematic policy of economic denial; one cannot easily comprehend the *Journal's* sardonic editorial statement that "We sympathize and understand why they [". . . armchair Marxists around the world . . ."] now blame the United States. . . ." Isn't the *Journal* struck by the fact that, although every year during the Allende period Chile asked the United States for grain credits, within a few days after its overthrow, the military junta was awarded eight times the amount that Chile had received in the preceding three years? And just the other day the flood of private credits began once again, with Manufacturers Hanover leading the file of U.S. banks that are providing the military junta with $150 million of private credit. Another compelling fact is that the Inter-American Development Bank, which operates under a virtual U.S. veto, turned down every request made by the Allende government, but is now about to award the junta a development loan almost five times the amount of IDB's disbursements to Chile during the entire Allende period.

Martin's Chile was a hermetic world, with its base in the American-flavored Carrera Hotel and largely cut off from the political realities of the nation about which he was critically reporting. Martin is a man of cheerful loquacity. He arrived in Latin America for the first time in 1971, and came upon a Chile under Allende. One of his early and consistent tutors there has been Orlando Saenz, president of the Chilean Manufacturers Association. His interpreters were at best members of the right-wing faction of the Christian Democratic Party. When he entered slums he was escorted by a militant of the same faction and talked to dissident PDC-leaning members of the community. When he went into the countryside, he was on occasion the guest of expropriated estate owners. To some degree that caricatures his actual performance, but during the time we were both in Chile, that tended to be his *modus operandi*. The whole of Chile isn't opened up by that type of scrutiny.

Martin's characteristic style is to relate anecdotally a series of interviews with unnamed people who are predominantly critics of the former government. From such sources he documents his impression that post-junta Chile has "an almost unreal air of relaxed normality." A businessman tells him that the workers were showing up on the job even when they aren't scheduled, overlooking what he partially admits—that an atmosphere of fear and insecurity pervades the working classes. He then drifts over to Santiago's Cafe Haiti (a gathering place for businessmen and professionals), where he gets in conversation with an unnamed Communist engineer who expands freely on the corruption and lack of discipline of Allende's Chile. Back at the foreign ministry, Martin discovers former staffers who are almost grateful for being fired by the new regime. As for the casualties at the Universidad Tecnico de Estado on the day of the coup, he discounts the "reports in the foreign press of mass killings," because "the death toll in this incident has since been revised to twenty, most of whom were reportedly foreign revolutionaries registered as students." But where, other than in a junta press release, could one find these "revised" figures, and who reported that "foreign revolutionaries" were registered as students? A Chilean student who attended that university and who is a member of the Frei faction of the PDC has assured me that upwards of seventy-five students and others were killed in that incident. One of Martin's major shortcomings is that he finds it easy to believe junta press releases, and equally difficult to believe statements from sources favorable to the former Allende government.

I do not dismiss that government's many errors of administration and conceptualization of policy. The record of such mistakes is substantial, and I have commented on it elsewhere. Nor do I want to debate Pablo Huneeus' thoroughly consistent opposition to the Allende government from its inception. Nor is it my intent to dwell on Martin's careless and naive reportage (naive, certainly not conspiratorial), nor his inability to deal maturely and adequately with what he accurately calls "one of the most complex nations in the world."

What does concern me is the breezy way in which Martin and the editorial board of *The Wall Street Journal* have become militant apologists for a military regime that fulfills in every respect the definition of the word totalitarian, if not fascistic. I would have, for example, expected the *Journal* and its staff to display some concern for freedom of the press in Chile, some concern for civil liberties and civil rights and some ability to separate themselves from an attitude which tacitly assumes that the only segment of Chile worth concern is the middle class, and that the main yardstick of a nation's achievement is its GNP.

The quality of Everett Martin's reportage is particularly important because *The Wall Street Journal* is one of a handful of American newspapers that has a specifically designated correspondent for the Latin American area. It is essential, at a time when the region is experiencing a rising level of economic and political nationalism, that the U.S. business community be accurately informed of the problems and expectations of Latin America. Everett Martin's coverage of the Chile story patently fails in that respect. It would seem, also, that in a period of East-West detente, he reveals a certain lack of sophistication by constantly employing variants of the phrase, "the Marxist government of Chile." How would we respond if the left-wing press in other countries used the phrase, "the capitalist government of the United States?" Rather than mocking the effort being made by the U.S. academic community to grasp what has been occurring in Chile, it might be constructive if correspondents like Martin joined the scholars in a mutual learning process. The collaboration might improve our comprehension of a region which, when it receives any attention at all in the American press, all too often suffers from the biases of the reporters operating in the field.

Few recent international incidents have witnessed such a regrettable journalistic performance as *The Wall Street Journal's* coverage of Chile. Perhaps the phrase—"underlying contempt for Chile"—which Huneeus uses to score his opponents, should be redirected toward his employer: the *Journal's* treatment of the Allende years and the aftermath is almost a case history in distortion, ill will, condescension and amateurism.

Everett Martin Responds

EVERETT G. MARTIN

The following exchange of letters took place in the January 19, 1974 issue of the Nation.

Professor Laurence Birns in his effort to discredit Chilean sociologist Pablo Huneeus and myself seems to have had considerable difficulty staying within the bounds of accuracy. Some examples:

Mr. Huneeus is *not* a member of the right wing faction of the Christian Democrats. Although he held an appointed post in the Frei government, he's never been a member of any political party.

He has never criticized Dr. Allende on television. His last TV appearance was in 1970 on a panel discussion about youth while he was a U.N. employee.

Mr. Huneeus' so-called "extended honeymoon in the Spanish Mediterranean" was actually time spent working on a research project under the auspices of the sociological institute of Madrid University. He produced a book called *The Bureaucrats,* a look at how a state functions, and completed research for a second book on the Spanish young generation.

Far from being a "Chilean Joyce Brothers" in a woman's magazine, at age 33 he has to his credit 17 papers for technical journals and three books: *Social Situation of Copper Miners* ('69), *Human Resources and Em-*

ployment Policy ('70), and *The Bureaucrats.* The first two, at least, are sufficiently dull to satisfy scholarly standards.

Rather than having contact with only the upper classes, as Mr. Birns claims, Mr. Huneeus is known for his field research. He lived for three months with miners for his copper study and the work brought about new laws to protect them from exploitation. For three years he was director of the National Employment Service, which brought him in close daily contact with the unemployed. A fellow correspondent two years ago told me Mr. Huneeus was *the* best single source to contact in Chile. That correspondent was John Barnes of *Newsweek.*

I have never written or held the conclusion "that a majority of the public (in Chile) advocated the violent, bloody overthrow of the constitutional government," as Mr. Birns writes.

I've never been the guest of an expropriated landlord. I don't even know one and I consider this to be a short-coming since I should have contacts at all levels of Chilean society.

Dean Jaime del Valle of the Catholic University Law School says he did not back away from his charges of election fraud, as Mr. Birns wrote. In fact, he reported on television that votes cast in the March election exceeded possible voters by 250,000, or 8 per cent of the total vote.

In allowing Mr. Huneeus space to argue against the *Newsweek* story, "Slaughterhouse in Santiago," *The Wall Street Journal* is not supporting the coup, nor denying that there was killing nor approving of killing. But, as Mr. Birns notes, the *Newsweek* account was the most influential coming from Santiago; and by all that I and other correspondents could learn, it was gross overstatement.

Jonathan Kandell of *The New York Times* and Lewis Diuguid of *The Washington Post* each independently wrote stories casting substantial doubt on the *Newsweek* account. Mr. Kandell found that in Pincoya poblacion, where Mr. Barnes reported that all males in one square block were killed, in fact only one person had died. He also found, as Mr. Huneeus did, that the morgue figures were for the period since January one and not for the first two weeks of the coup.

The difference between Mr. Birns and myself arises because I am only a reporter, not an advocate of any kind of ideology. What I found in Chile determined what I wrote. In defense of my stories I can only say that our readers were informed that the Allende government was heading into serious trouble and that the climax was likely to come this year.

Mr. Birns' central complaint against my reporting can be discerned when he quotes himself as having written in *The New York Review of Books*, "Mr. Martin's reportage on Chile is helping to 'construct a mythology designed to show that Allende was responsible for his own fall.'" The facts reported in my articles are uncomfortable to Mr. Birns' romantic preconceptions. As a result, although he was not in Chile during or after the coup, he sets out to "correct" those facts through personal attacks which are themselves laced with inaccuracies.

Laurence Birns Responds to Everett Martin

Mr. Martin speaks about my "inaccuracies," yet he is reluctant about citing them. In my article I had listed a number of major points and fact after fact where he had erred. In his letter, he mentions not one of them, nor does he refer to my support of Prof. Bradford Burns's estimate of the size of a pro-Allende parade, which was the very *raison d'etre* of Mr. Martin's November 2nd *Wall Street Journal* article. Even then I had decided not to quote from Mr. Martin's column of October 24, 1972 because I feared that his employer might start asking embarrassing questions of him. This article included the sentence, "And the President [Allende] himself isn't up for re-election until 1976." Of course, the Chilean constitution does not permit re-election of an incumbent President.

He contents himself to rebut what I myself had described as symbolic conjecturings: that he had spent his time largely in Chile with the middle class. I still insist that this is the case. I agree with Mr. Martin that he ". . . should have contacts at all levels of Chilean society." But the question is, did he? As for the visit to the expropriated landlord, he might never have reached the *fundo* but it was certainly his intention to make the trip.

In my article I made the claim that I can cite at least eighty-five instances where Mr. Martin was factually incorrect or produced distorted interpretations of events. My claim remains. If the *Journal* will provide the space to do this I will gladly oblige.

Concerning Mr. Huneeus, I stand on the account of his professional and political evaluation that was developed in my article. To those who know him, Huneeus always identified himself with the PDC and spoke as if he were a member. The greater fact is that Mr. Huneeus is a minor personality in Chilean national and intellectual life and for Mr. Martin to suggest that he is a man of the people is simply mirthful. For the *Journal* to peg so much on Huneeus' analysis is in itself a reflection upon the paucity of insight that it has shown regarding Chile.

Concerning the del Valle charges about alleged electoral fraud (I call them concoctions) in the congressional election, my differences were not with the dean. I was taking issue with Mr. Martin's original *Journal* report that there was "mounting evidence that there was considerable fraud. . . ." A more professional way for Martin to have presented his evidence would have been to have specifically cited del Valle as his one source, characterize the dean's position in the Chilean intellectual community, and then present contrary evidence, if any existed. I say that overwhelmingly the evidence was to the contrary. Mr. Martin says that ". . .*The Wall Street Journal* is not supporting the coup, not denying that there was killing nor approving of killing." But isn't this statement testing our gullibility? If the opposite isn't true then why did Mr. Martin call those who opposed the junta "resisters" rather than constitutionalists, and why does he cite Allende as the man who "defied" the military rather than the military which was defying the lawful President.

But if the above contains something of interest, it has to be subsidiary to Mr. Martin's suggestion that the difference between him and myself is that "I [Martin] am only a reporter, not an advocate of any kind of ideology." Mr. Martin would like to think of himself as "only a reporter," an honest man in a dishonest world. But why then does he title one of his articles "Wrecking Chile to Build Marxism"? Ideology is not only the possession of the left. Self-identified middle-roaders too have their ideology. During the period of his reporting, he consistently ridiculed and denigrated the policies and institutions of the Allende administration, in contrast to the image of solidarity and efficiency which he attributed to those who opposed it. As for his self-identified service in informing his readers that things were in bad shape in Chile before the overthrow, one needn't be a Pulitzer candidate to have had this insight. There wasn't a newspaperman or newspaper within or without Chile who wasn't saying precisely this. Perhaps a more significant service to a readership would have been telling why this was so, and what were the constellation of forces producing Chile's parlous state, and what were the options open to the government and opposition leaderships, and what were the external and internal constraints acting upon them. Mr. Martin never provides us with this type of analysis. In fact, he never analyzes, but merely presents a series of semi-amusing, if tinted, vignettes, carefully constructed to present a dogma out of which we are meant to extrapolate major political judgments. As for the *Journal's* editorials, its finding that "The generals took care of him [Allende] before he and his assassination crews could get to them," respects neither facts nor any pretense to fairness.

The reason why I undertook this investigation of Martin's reportage is not, as he states, because the "facts reported in my articles are uncomfortable to Mr. Birns's romantic preconceptions." After experiencing the realities of Allende's rule, the quality of the opposition, and scrutinizing the operation of the military junta after the coup, it is difficult to be romantic about Chile. What troubles me is that Martin's "facts" often turn out to be nonfacts, and that the language that he uses, the themes that he selected to write about, the vignettes that he presented, and the explanations that he provided *consistently* could have been straight from the manual of arms of the nation's right wing. I am saying that his has been poor reporting which falls apart once it is closely analyzed and assessed. In my article, I had spelled out my charges. Mr. Martin chooses not to respond to them.